Richard Le Gallienne

Prose Fancies

Richard Le Gallienne

Prose Fancies

ISBN/EAN: 9783744685979

Printed in Europe, USA, Canada, Australia, Japan

Cover: Foto ©Thomas Meinert / pixelio.de

More available books at **www.hansebooks.com**

Prose Fancies

by
Richard Le Gallienne

With portrait

New York: *G. P. Putnam's Sons, 27 W. Twenty-third St.* London: *Elkin Mathews and John Lane: 1899*

TO

MY DEAR WIFE

MY PROSE FOR HER POETRY

IN MEMORY

OF TWO HAPPY YEARS

OCTOBER 22, 1891

DECEMBER 6

1893

CONTENTS

A SPRING MORNING

SPRING puts the old pipe to his lips and blows a note or two. At the sound, little thrills pass across the wintry meadows. The bushes are dotted with innumerable tiny sparks of green, that will soon set fire to the whole hedgerow; here and there they have gone so far as those little tufts which the children call 'bread and cheese.' A gentle change is coming over the grim avenue of the elms yonder. They won't relent so far as to admit buds, but there is an unmistakable bloom upon them, like the promise of a smile. The rooks have known it for some weeks, and already their Jews' market is in full caw. The more complaisant chestnut dandles its sticky knobs.

A

Soon they will be brussels-sprouts, and then
they will shake open their fairy umbrellas.
So says a child of my acquaintance. The
water-lilies already poke their green scrolls
above the surface of the pond, a few buttercups venture into the meadows, but daisies
are still precious as asparagus. The air
is warm as your love's cheek, golden as
canary. It is all a-clink and a-glitter, it
trills and chirps on every hand. Somewhere close by, but unseen, a young man is
whistling at his work ; and, putting your ear
to the ground, you shall hear how the earth
beneath is alive with a million little beating
hearts. *C'est l'heure exquise.*

Presently along the road comes slowly,
and at times erratically, a charming procession. Following the fashion, or even setting
it, three weeks since yon old sow budded.
From her side, recalling the Trojan horse,
sprang suddenly a little company of black-
and-tan piglets, fully legged and snouted for
the battle of life. She is taking them with
her to put them to school at a farm two or
three miles away. So I understand her.
They surround her in a compact body, ever

moving and poking and squeaking, yet all
keeping together.   As they advance slowly,
she towering above her tiny bodyguard, one
thinks of Gulliver moving through Lilliput ;
and there is a touch of solemnity in the
procession which recalls a mighty Indian
idol being carried through the streets, with
people thronging about its feet.   How delicately she steps, lest she hurt one of the little
limbs!   And, meanwhile, mark the driver—
for though the old pig pretends to ignore any
such coercion, as men believe in free-will,
yet there is a fate, a driver, to this idyllic
domestic company.   But how gentle is he
too!   He never lets it be seen that he is
driving them.   He carries a little switch,
rather, it would appear, for form's sake ; for
he seldom does more with it than tickle the
gravely striding posteriors of the quaint
little people.   He is wise as he is kind,
for he knows that he is driving quicksilver.
The least undue coercion, the least sudden
start, and they will be off like spilled
marbles, in eleven different directions.   Sometimes occasion arises for prompt action :
when the poet of the family dreams he

discerns the promised land through the bottom of a gate, and is bent on squeezing his way under, and the demoralisation of the whole eleven seems imminent. Then, unconsciously applying the wisdom of Solomon, the driver deals a smart flick to the old mother. Seeing her move on, and reflecting that she carries all the provisions of the party, her children think better of their romance, and gambol after her, taking a gamesome pull at her teats from high spirits.

The man never seems to get angry with them. He is smiling gently to himself all the time, as he softly and leisurely walks behind them. Indeed, wherever this moving nursery of young life passes, it awakens tenderness. The man who drove the gig so rapidly a little way off suddenly slows down, and, with a sympathetic word, walks his horse gingerly by. Every pedestrian stops and smiles, and on every face comes a transforming tenderness, a touch of almost motherly sweetness. So dear is young life to the eye and heart of man.

A few weeks hence these same pedestrians

will pass these same pigs with no emotion, beyond, possibly, that produced by the sweet savour of frying ham. Their *naïveté*, their charming baby quaintness, will have departed for ever. Their features, as yet but roguishly indicated, will have become set and hidebound ; their soft little snouts will be ringed, and hard as a fifth hoof; their dainty little ears—veritable silk purses —will have grown long and bristly : in short, they will have lost that ineffable tender bloom of young life which makes them quite a touching sight to-day. Strange that loss of charm which comes with development in us all, pigs included. A tendency to pigginess, as in these youngsters, a tendency to manhood in the prattling and crowing babe, are both hailed as charming: but the full-grown pig! the full-grown man! Alas! in each case the charm seems to flee with the advent of bristles.

But let us return to the driver.

Under his arm he carries a basket, from which now and again proceed suppressed squeaks and grunts. It is 'the rickling,' the weakling, of the family. It will pro-

bably find an early death, and be embalmed
in sage and onions. The man has already
had an offer for it—from 'Mr. Lamb.' Mr.
Lamb! Yes, Mr. Lamb at Six-Elm Farm.
'Oh! I see.' But was it not a startling
coincidence?

It has taken half an hour to come from
the old bridge to the cross-roads, barely
half a mile. And now, good-bye, funny
little silken-coated piglets; good-bye, grave
old mother. Ge-whoop! Good-bye, gentle
driver. As you move behind your charge
with that tender smile, with that burden
safely pressed beneath your arm, I seem
to have had a vision of the Good Shepherd.

II

Down by the river there is, as yet, little
sign of spring. Its bed is all choked with
last year's reeds, trampled about like a
manger. Yet its running seems to have
caught a happier note, and here and there
along its banks flash silvery wands of palm.
Right down among the shabby burnt-out
underwood moves the sordid figure of a

man. He seems the very *genius loci*. His clothes are torn and soiled, as though he had slept on the ground. The white lining of one arm gleams out like the slashing in a doublet. His hat is battered, and he wears no collar. I don't like staring at his face, for he has been unfortunate. Yet a glimpse tells me that he is far down the hill of life, old and drink-corroded at fifty. He is miserably gathering sticks—perhaps a little job for the farm close by. He probably slept in the barn there last night, turned out drunk from the public-house. He will probably do and be done by likewise to-night. How many faggots to the dram? one wonders. What is he thinking as he rustles about disconsolately among the bushes? Of what is he *dreaming*? What does he make of the lark up there? But I notice he never looks at it. Perhaps he cannot bear to. For who knows what is in the heart beneath that poor soiled coat? If you have hopes, he may have memories. Some day your hopes will be memories too—birds that have flown away, flowers long since withered.

III

A short way further along, I come across
a boy gathering palm. He is a town boy,
and has come all the way from Whitechapel
thus early. He has already gathered a
great bundle—worth five shillings to him,
he says. This same palm will to-morrow
be distributed over London, and those who
buy sprigs of it by the Bank will know
nothing of the blue-eyed boy who gathered
it, and the murmuring river by which it
grew. And the lad, once more lost in some
squalid court, will be a sort of Sir John
Mandeville to his companions—a Sir John
Mandeville of the fields, with their water-rats,
their birds' eggs, and many other wonders.
And one can imagine him saying, 'And the
sparrows there fly right up into the sun, and
sing like angels!' But he won't get his
comrades to believe *that*.

IV

Spring has a wonderful way of bringing
out hidden traits of character. Through my
window I look out upon a tiny farm. It is

kept by a tall, hard-looking, rough-bearded fellow, whom I have watched striding about his fields all winter, with but little sympathy. Yet it would seem I have been doing him wrong. For this morning, as he passed along the outside of the railing wherein his two sheep were grazing, suddenly they came bounding towards him with every manifestation of delight, literally recalling the lambkins which Wordsworth saw bound 'as to the tabor's sound.' They followed as far as the railing permitted, pushing their noses through at him ; nay, when at last he moved out of reach, they were evidently so much in love that they leaped the fence and made after him. And he, instead of turning brutally on them, as I had expected, smiled and played with them awhile. Indeed, he had some difficulty in disengaging himself from their persistent affection. So, evidently, they knew him better than I.

A CONSPIRACY OF SILENCE

WHY do we go on talking? It is a serious question, one on which the happiness of thousands depends. For there is no more wearing social demand than that of compulsory conversation. All day long we must either talk, or—dread alternative—listen. Now, that were very well if we had something to say, or our fellow-sufferer something to tell, or, best of all, if either of us possessed the gift of clothing the old commonplaces with charm. But men with that great gift are not to be met with in every railway-carriage, or at every dinner. The man we actually meet is one whose joke, though we have signalled it a mile off, we are powerless to stop, whose opinions come out with a whirr as of clockwork. Besides, it always happens in life that the man—or woman—with whom we would like to talk is

10

at the next table. Those who really have something to say to each other so seldom have a chance of saying it.

Why, O why, do we go on talking? We ask the question in all seriousness, not merely in the hope of making some cheap paradoxical fun out of the answer. It is a cry from the deeps of ineffable boredom.

Is it to impart information? At the best it is a dreary ideal. But, at any rate, it is a mistaken use of the tongue, for there is no information we can impart which has not been far more accurately stated in book-form. Even if it should happen to be a quite new fact, an accident happily rare as the transit of Venus—a new fact about the North Pole, for instance—well, a book, not a conversation, is the place for it. To talk book, past, present, or to come, is not to converse.

To converse, as with every other art, is out of three platitudes to make not a fourth platitude—'but a star.' Newness of information is no necessity of conversation: else were the Central News Agency the best of talkers. Indeed, the oldest information is

perhaps the best material for the artist as
talker: though, truly, as with every other
artist, material matters little. There are
just two or three men of letters left to us,
who provide us examples of that inspired
soliloquy, those conversations of one, which
are our nearest approach to the talk of other
days. How good it is to listen to one of
these!—for it is the great charm of their talk
that we remember nothing. There were no
prickly bits of information to stick on one's
mind like burrs. Their talk had no regular
features, but, like a sunrise, was all music
and glory.

The friend who talks the night through
with his friend, till the dawn climbs in like a
pallid rose at the window; the lovers who,
while the sun is setting, sit in the greenwood
and say, 'Is it thou? It is I!' in awestruck
antiphony, till the stars appear; and, holiest
converse of all, the mystic prattle of mother
and babe: why are all these such wonderful talk if not because we remember no
word of them — only the glory? They
leave us nothing, in image worthy of the
time, to 'pigeon-hole,' nothing to store

with our vouchers in the 'pigeon-holes' of memory.

Pigeon-holes of memory! Think of the degradation. And memory was once a honeycomb, a hive of all the wonderful words of poets, of all the marvellous moods of lovers. Once it was a shell that listened tremulously upon Olympus, and caught the accents of the Gods; now it is a phono- graph catching every word that falleth from the mouths of the board of guardians. Once a muse, now a servile drudge 'twixt man and man.

And this 'pigeon-hole' memory—once an impressionist of divine moments, now the miser of all unimportant, trivial detail—is our tyrant, the muse of modern talk. Men talk now not what they feel or think, but what they remember, with their bad good memories. If they remembered the poets, or their first love, or the spring, or the stars, it were well enough: but no! they remember but what the poets ate and wore, the last divorce case, the state of the crops, the last trivial detail about Mars. The man with the muck-rake would have made a great reputation as a talker had he lived to-day : for, as our modern speech has it, a Great Man simply means a Great Memory, and a Great Memory is simply a prosperous marine-store.

What, in fact, do we talk about? Mainly about our business, our food, or our diseases. All three themes more or less centre in that of food. How we revel in the brutal digestive details, and call it gastronomy! How our host plumes himself on his wine, as though it were a personal virtue, and not the merely obvious accessory of a man with ten thousand a year! Strange, is it not, how we pat and stroke our possessions as though they belonged to us, instead of to our money —our grandfather's money?

There is, some hope and believe, an imminent Return to Simplicity—Socialism the unwise it call. If it be really true, what good news for the grave humorous man, who hates talking to anything but trees and children! For, if that Return to Simplicity means anything, it must mean the sweeping away of immemorial rookeries of talk—such crannied hives of gossip as the professions, with all their garrulous heritage of trivial

witty *ana*: literary, dramatic, legal, aristocratic, ecclesiastical, commercial.   How good
to dip them all deep in the great ocean of
oblivion, and watch the bookworms, diarists,
'raconteurs,' and all the old-clothesmen of life,
scurrying out of their holes, as when in
summer-time Mary Anne submerges the cock-
roach trap within the pail!   And O, let there
be no Noah to that flood!   Let none survive
to tell another tale; for, only when the
chronicler of small-beer is dead, shall we be
able to know men as men, heroes as heroes,
poets as poets—instead of mere centres of
gossip, an inch of text to a yard of footnote.
Then only may we begin to talk of something worth the talking: not merely of how
the great man creased his trousers, and call it
'the study of character,' but of how he was
great, and whether it is possible to climb
after him.

Talk, too, is so definite, so limited.   The
people we meet might seem so wonderful,
might mean such quaint and charming
meanings sometimes, if they would not
talk.   Like some delightfully bound old
volume in a foreign tongue, that looks like

one of the Sibylline books, till a friend
translates the title and explains that it is
a sixteenth-century law dictionary: so are
the men and women we meet. How interesting they might be if they would not
persist in telling us what they are about!

That, indeed, is the abiding charm of
Nature. No sensible man can envy Asylas,
to whom the language of birds was as
familiar as French *argot* to our young
décadents. Think how terrible it would be
if Nature could all of a sudden learn
English! That exquisite mirror of all our
shifting moods would be broken for ever.
No longer might we coin the woodland
into metaphors of our own joys and sorrows.
The birds would no longer flute to us of
lost loves, but of found worms; we should
realise how terribly selfish they are; we
could never more quote 'Hark, hark, the
lark at heaven's gate sings,' or poetise with
Mr. Patmore of 'the heavenly-minded thrush.'
And what awful voices some of those great
red roses would have! Yes, Nature is so
sympathetic because she is so silent ; because,
when she does talk, she talks in a language

which we cannot understand, but only guess at ; and her silence allows us to hear her eternal meanings, which her gossiping would drown.

Happy monks of La Trappe! One has heard the foolish chattering world take pity upon you. An hour of talk to a year of silence! O heavenly proportion! And I can well imagine that when that hour has come, it seems but a trivial toy you have forgotten how to play with. Were I a Trappist, I would use my hour to evangelise converts to silence, would break the long year's quiet but to whisper, 'How good is silence!' Let us inaugurate a secular La Trappe, let us plot a conspiracy of silence, let us send the world to Coventry. Or, if we must talk, let it be in Latin, or in the 'Volapük' of myriad-meaning music ; and let no man joke save in Greek—that all may laugh. But, best of all, let us leave off talking altogether, and listen to the morning stars.

LIFE IN INVERTED COMMAS

As I waited for an omnibus at the corner of
Fleet Street the other day, I was the spectator of a curious occurrence. Suddenly
there was a scuffle hard by me, and, turning
round, I saw a powerful gentlemanly man
wrestling with two others in livery, who were
evidently intent on arresting him. These
men, I at once perceived, belonged to the
detective force of the Incorporated Society of
Authors, and were engaged in the capture of
a notorious plagiarist. I knew the prisoner
well. He had, in fact, pillaged from my own
writings ; but I was none the less sorry for
his plight, to which, I would assure the
reader, I was no party. Yet he was, I
admit, an egregiously bad case, and my pity
is doubtless misplaced sentiment. Like
many another, he had begun his career as a
quotation and ended as a plagiarism, daring

18

even, in one instance, to imitate that shadow in the fairy-tale, which rose up on a sudden one day and declared himself to be the substance and the substance his shadow. Indeed, he had so far succeeded as to make many people question whether or not he was the original and the other man the plagiarism. However, there was no longer to be any doubt of it, for his captors had him fast this time; and, presently, we saw him taken off in a hansom, well secured between strong inverted commas.

This curious circumstance set me reflecting, and, as we trundled along towards Charing Cross, my mind gave birth to sundry sententious reflections.

After all, I thought, that unlucky plagiarist is no worse than most of us : for is it not true that few of us live as conscientiously as we should within our inverted commas? We are far more inclined to live in that author, not ourselves, who makes for originality. It is, of course, difficult, even with the best intentions, to make proper acknowledgment of all our 'authorities'—to attach, so to say, the true '*del. et sculp.*' to all our

little bits of art. There is so much in our
lives that we honestly don't know how we
came by.

As I reflected in this wise, I was drawn to
notice my companions in the omnibus, and
lo! there was not an original person amongst
us. Yet I looked in vain to see if they wore
their inverted commas. Not one of them,
believe me, had had the honesty to bring
them. Each looked at me unblushingly, as
though he were really original, and not a
cheap German print of originals I had seen
in books and pictures since I could read.
I really think that they must have been
unaware of their imposture. They could
hardly have pretended so successfully.

There was the young dandy just let loose
from his band-box, wearing exactly the same
face, the same smile, the same neck-tie,
holding his stick in exactly the same fashion,
talking exactly the same words, with pre-
cisely the same accent, as his neighbour,
another dandy, and as all the other dandies
between the Bank and Hyde Park Corner.
Yet he seemed persuaded of his own originality. He evidently felt that there was

something individual about him, and apparently relied with confidence on his friend not addressing a third dandy by mistake for him. I hope he had his name safe in his hat.

Looking at these three examples of Nature's love of repeating herself, I said to myself: Somewhere in heaven stands a great stencil, and at each sweep of the cosmic brush a million dandies are born, each one alike as a box of collars. Indeed, I felt that this stencil process had been employed in the manufacture of every single person in that omnibus: two middle-aged matrons, each of whom seemed to think that having given birth to six children was an indisputable claim to originality ; two elderly business men to correspond ; a young miss carrying music and wearing eye-glasses ; and a clergyman discussing stocks with one of the business men ; I alone in my corner being, of course, the one occupant for whom Nature had been at the expense of casting a special mould, and at the extravagance of breaking it.

Presently a matron and a business man

alighted, and two dainty young women,
evidently of artistic tendencies, joined the
Hammersmith pilgrims.   One saw at a glance
that they were very sure of their originality.
There were no inverted commas around their
pretty young heads, bless them!   But then
Queen Anne houses are as much on a pattern
as more commonplace structures, and Bedford
Parkians are already being manufactured by
celestial stencil.   What I specially noticed
about them was their plagiarised voices—
curious, yearning things, evidently intended
to suggest depths of infinite passion, con-
trolled by many a wild and weary past,

> ‘ Infinite passion and the pain
> Of finite souls that yearn ’—

the kind of voice, you know, in which
Socialist actresses yearn out passages from
‘ The Cenci,’ feeling that they do a fearful
thing.   The voice began, I believe, with
Miss Ellen Terry.   With her, though, it is
charming, for it is, we feel, the voice of real
emotion.   There are real tears in it.   It is
her own.   But with these ladies, who were
discussing the last ‘ Independent ’ play, it

was so evidently a stop pulled out by
affectation—the *vox inhumana*, one might
say, for it is a voice unlike anything else to
be found in the four elements. It has its
counterpart in the imitators of Mr. Beerbohm
Tree—young actors who likewise endeavour
to make up for the lack of anything like
dramatic passion by pretending to control
it : the control being feigned by a set jaw or
a hard, throaty, uncadenced voice of preter-
natural solemnity. These ladies, too, wore
plagiarised gowns of the most 'original'
style, plagiarised hats, glittering plagiarised
smiles ; and yet they so evidently looked
down on every one else in the omnibus, whom,
perhaps, after all, it had been kinder of me
to describe as the hackneyed quotations of
humanity, who had probably thought it
unnecessary to wear their inverted commas,
as they were so well known.

At last I grew impatient of them, and,
leaving the omnibus, finished my journey
home by the Underground. What was my
surprise when I reached it to find our little
house wearing inverted commas—two on the
chimney, and two on the gate! My wife,

too ! and the words of endearing salutation
with which I greeted her, why, they also to
my diseased fancy seemed to leave my lips
between quotation marks.   There is nothing
in which we fancy ourselves so original as in
our terms of endearment, nothing in which
we are so like all the world ; for, alas ! there
is no euphuism of affection which lovers have
not prattled together in springtides long
before the Christian era.   If you call your
wife 'a chuck,' so did Othello; and, whatever
dainty diminutive you may hit on, Catullus,
with his warbling Latin, 'makes mouths at
our speech.'

I grew so haunted with this oppressive
thought, that my wife could not but notice
my trouble.   But how could I tell her of the
spectral inverted commas that dodged every
move of her dear head ?—tell her that our
own original firstborn, just beginning to talk
as never baby talked, was an unblushing
plagiarism of his great-great-great-grand-
father, that our love was nothing but the
expansion of a line of Keats, and that our
whole life was one hideous mockery of
originality ?   'Woman,' I felt inclined to

shriek, 'be yourself, and not your great-grandmother. A man may not marry his great-grandmother. For God's sake let us all be ourselves, and not ghastly mimicries of our ancestors, or our neighbours. Let us shake ourselves free from this evil dream of imitation. Merciful Heaven, it is killing me!' But surely that was a quotation too, and, accidentally catching sight of the back of my hand, suddenly the tears sprang to my eyes, for it was just so the big soft veins used to be on the hands of my father, when a little boy I prayed between his knees. He was gone, but here was his hand—*his* hand, not mine!

Then an idea possessed me. There was but one way. I could die. There was a little phial of laudanum in the medicine-cupboard that always leered at me from among the other bottles like a serpent's eye. Thrice happy thought! Who would miss such a poor imitation? Even the mere soap-vending tradesmen bid us 'beware of imitations.' Dark wine of forgetfulness. . . . No, that was a quotation. However, here was the phial. I drew the cork, inhaled for

a moment the hard dry odour of poppies,
and prepared to drink. But just at that
moment I seemed to hear a horrid little
laugh coming out of the bottle, and a voice
chuckled at my ear : 'You ass, do you call
that original'? It was so absurd that I
burst out into hysterical laughter. Here
had I been about to do the most 'banal'
thing of all. Was there anything in the
world quite so commonplace as suicide?

And with the good spirits of laughter
came peace. Nay, why worry to be 'original'?
Why such haste to be unlike the rest of the
world, when the best things of life were
manifestly those which all men had in
common? Was love less sweet because my
next-door neighbour knew it as well? Would
the same reason make death less bitter?
And were not those tender diminutives all
the more precious, because their vowels had
been rounded for us by the sweet lips of
lovers dead and gone?—sainted jewels, still
warm from the beat of tragic bosoms, flowers
which their kisses had freighted with immortal meanings.

And then I bethought me how the

meadow-daisies were one as the other, and how, when the pearly shells of the dog rose settled on the hedge like a flight of butter-flies, one was as the other; how the birds sang alike, how star was twin with star, and in peas is no distinction. My rhetoric stopped as I was about to say 'as wife is to wife'—for I thought I would first kiss her and see: and lo! I was once more perplexed, for as I looked down into her eyes, simple and blue and deep, as the sky is simple and blue and deep, I declared her to be the only woman in the world—which was obviously not exact. But it was true, for all that.

FRACTIONAL HUMANITY

MANKIND, in its heavy fashion, has chosen to mock the tailor with the fact—the indubitable fact—that he is but the ninth part of a man. Yet, after all, at this time of day, it seems more of a compliment than a gibe. To be a whole ninth of a man! Few of us, when we ponder it, can boast so much. Take, for instance, that other proverbial case of the fractional-part-of-a-pin-maker. It takes nine persons to make a pin, we were taught in our catechism. Actually that means that it takes nine persons to make one whole pin-maker, which leaves the question still to be solved as to how many whole pin-makers it takes to make a man. What is the relation of one pin-maker to the whole social economy? That discovered, a multiplication by nine will give us the exact fractional part of manhood which belongs to the ninth-of-a-pin-maker. Obviously he is a much more microscopic creature than the immemorially despised tailor, and, alas ! his case is nearest that of most of us. And it is curious to notice how we rejoice in, rather than lament, this inevitable result of that great law of differentiation, which one may figure as a terrible machine hour after hour chopping up mankind into more and more infinitesimal fragments. We feel a pride in being spoken of as 'specialists'—and yet what is a specialist ? The nine-hundred-and-ninety-ninth part of a man. Call me not an entomologist, call me a lepidopterist, if you will—though, really, that is too broad a term for a man who is not so much taken up with moths generally as with the third ring of the antennæ of the great oak-eggar.

If one is troubled with a gift for symbolism, it is hard to treat any man one meets as though he were really a whole man : to treat a lawyer as though he were anything but a deed of assignment, or a surgeon as if he were anything more than an operation. As the metropolitan trains load and unload in a morning, what does one see ? Gross upon

gross of steel pens, a few quills, whole
carriages full of bricklayers' trowels, and how
strange it seems to watch all the bank-books
sorting themselves out from the motley, and
arranging themselves in the first classes, just
as we see them on the shelf in the bank. It
is a curious sight. The little shop-girl there,
what is she but a roll of pink ribbon?—nay,
she is but half-a-yard. And the poor infinitesimal porters and guards, how pathetically
small seems their share in the great mono-
syllable Man, animalcules in that great
social system which, again, is but an animal-
cule in the blood of Time. Still more infinitesimal seems the man who is a subdivision,
not of a form of work even, but merely of a
form of taste ; the man who collects foreign
stamps, say, or book-plates, or arrow-heads,
the connoisseur of a tiny section of one of the
lesser schools of Italian painting, the coral-
insect who has devoted his life to a participle,
first-edition men, and all those various bookworms who, without impropriety be it
spoken, are the maggots that breed in the
dung of the great. A certain friend of mine
always appears to me in the similitude of a

first edition of one of Mr. Hardy's novels.
I have the greatest difficulty at times to
prevent myself forcibly setting him upon my
shelf to complete my set ; for, oddly enough,
he is the one bit of Hardyana I lack. In
which confession I let the reader into the
secret of my own petty limitations. To have
one's horizon bounded by a book-plate, to
have no hope, no wish in life, beyond a first
edition ! The workers, however sectional,
have some place in the text of the great
book of life, but such mere testers and tasters
of existence have hardly a place even in the
gloss, though it be printed in the most
microscopic diamond.

And every moment, as we said, we are
being turned out smaller and smaller from
the mill of Time. You ask your little boy
what he would like to be when he grows
up. To your consternation he answers, ' A
man !' You hide your face : you cannot tell
him how impossible it is now to be that.
Poor little chap ! He is born centuries too
late. You cannot promise even that he
shall be a tailor, for by the time he is old
enough to be apprenticed, how do you know

how that ancient profession may be divided
up? May you not have sadly to tell him :
'My poor boy, it is impossible to make you
that—for there are no longer any whole-
tailors. You may, if you like, be a thread-
waxer or a needle-threader ; you may be one
of the thirty men it takes to make a button-
hole, but a complete tailor—alas! it is
impossible.'

Who will save us from this remorseless
law of eternal subdivision? To make one
complete man out of all this vast collection of
snips and snippets of humanity. To piece
all the trades, professions, and fads together,
like a puzzle, till one saw the honest face of
a genuine man round and whole once more.
To take these dry bones of the Valley of
Commerce, and powerfully breathe into
them the unifying breath of life, that once
more they stand up, not as fractional bones
of the wrist or the ankle of manhood, but
mighty, full-blooded men as of old. Ah!
we must wait for a new creation for that.

The mystics have a suggestive fancy that
all our vast complex life once existed as a
peaceful unit in the mind of God. But

as God, brooding in the abyss, meditated upon Himself, various thoughts separated themselves and revolved within the atmosphere of His mind, at first unconscious of themselves or each other. Presently, desire of separate existence awoke in these shadowy things, a lust of corporeality grew upon them, and hence at last the fall into physical life, the realisation in concrete form of their diaphanous individualities. And that original cause of man's separation from deity, this desire of subdivision, how it has gone on operating, more and more! We call it differentiation, but the mystic would describe it as dividing ourselves more and more from God, the primeval unity in which alone is blessedness. Blake in one of his prophetic books sings man's 'fall into Division and his resurrection into Unity.' And when we look about us and consider but the common use of words, how do we find the mystic's apparently wild fancy illustrated in every section of our commonplace lives. What do we mean when we speak of 'division' of interests, 'division' of families, when we say that 'union' is strength, or

how good it is to dwell together in ' unity,'
or speak of lives 'made one'? Are we
not unwittingly expressing the unconscious
yearning of the fractions to merge once more
in the sweet kinship of the unit, of the ninths
and the nine-hundred-and-ninety-ninths of
humanity to merge their differences in the
mighty generalisation Man, of man to merge
his finite existence in the mysterious infinite,
the undivided, indivisible One, to 'be made
one,' as theology phrases it, ' with God '?
How the complex life of our time longs to
return to its first happy state of simplicity,
we feel on every hand. What is Socialism
but a vast throb of man's desire after unity?
We are overbred. The simple old type of
manhood is lost long since in endless orchid-
aceous variation. O! to be simple shepherds,
simple sailors, simple delvers of the soil, to
be something complete on our own account,
to be relative to nothing save God and His
stars!

THE WOMAN'S HALF-PROFITS

O ma pauvre Muse! est-ce toi?

FAME in Athens and Florence took the form of laurel, in London it is represented by 'Romeikes.' Hyacinth Rondel, the very latest new poet, sat one evening not long ago in his elegant new chambers, with a cloud of those pleasant witnesses about him, as charmed by 'the rustle' of their 'loved Apollian leaves' as though they had been veritable laurel or veritable bank-notes. His rooms were provided with all those distinguished comforts and elegancies proper to a success that may any moment be interviewed. Needless to say, the walls had been decorated by Mr. Whistler, and there was not a piece of furniture in the room that had not belonged to this or that poet deceased. Priceless autograph portraits of all the leading actors and actresses littered

35

the mantelshelf with a reckless prodigality,
the two or three choice etchings were, of
course, no less conspicuously inscribed to
their illustrious confrère by the artists—
naturally, the very latest hatched in Paris.
There was hardly a volume in the elegant
Chippendale bookcases not similarly inscribed.   Mr. Rondel would as soon have
thought of buying a book as of paying for a
stall.   To the eye of imagination, therefore,
there was not an article in the room which
did not carry a little trumpet to the distinguished poet's honour and glory.   Hidden
from view in his buhl cabinet, but none the
less vivid to his sensitive egoism, were those
tenderer trophies of his power, spoils of the
chase, which the adoring feminine had
offered up at his shrine: all his love-letters
sorted in periods, neatly ribboned and
snugly ensconced in various sandalwood
niches—much as urns are ranged at the
Crematorium, Woking—with locks of hair of
many hues.   He loved most to think of
those letters in which the women had gladly
sought a spiritual suttee, and begged him to
cement the stones of his temple of fame with

the blood of their devoted hearts. To have had a share in building so distinguished a life—that was enough for them! They asked no such inconvenient reward as marriage: indeed, one or two of them had already obtained that boon from others. To serve their purpose, and then, if it must be, to be forgotten, or—wild hope—to be em· balmed in a sonnet sequence: that was reward enough.

In the midst of this. silent and yet so eloquent orchestra, which from morn to night was continually crying 'Glory, glory, glory' in the ear of the self-enamoured poet, Hyacinth Rondel was sitting one evening. The last post had brought him the above-mentioned leaves of the Romeike laurel, and he sat in his easiest chair by the bright fire, adjusting them, metaphorically, upon his high brow, a decanter at his right-hand and cigarette smoke curling up from his left. At last he had drained all the honey from the last paragraph, and, with rustling shining head, he turned a sweeping triumphant gaze around his room. But, to his surprise, he found himself no longer alone. Was it the

Muse in dainty modern costume and delicately tinted cheek? Yes! it was one of those discarded Muses who sometimes remain upon the poet's hands as Fates.

When she raised her veil she certainly looked more of a Fate than a Muse. Her expression was not agreeable. The poet, afterwards describing the incident and remembering his Dante, spoke of her in an allegorical sonnet as 'lady of terrible aspect,' and symbolized her as Nemesis.

He now addressed her as 'Annette,' and in his voice were four notes of exclamation. She came closer to him, and very quietly, but with an accent that was the very quintessence of Ibsenism, made the somewhat mercantile statement: 'I have come for my half-profits!'

'Half-profits! What do you mean? Are you mad?'

'Not in the least! I want my share in the profits of all this pretty poetry,' and she contemptuously ran her fingers over the several slim volumes on the poet's shelves which represented his own contribution to English literature.

Rondel began to comprehend, but he was as yet too surprised to answer.

'Don't you understand?' she went on. ' It takes two to make poetry like yours—

> "They steal their song the lips that sing
> From lips that only kiss and cling."

Do you remember? Have I quoted correctly? Yes, here it is!' taking down a volume entitled *Liber Amoris*, the passionate confession which had first brought the poet his fame. As a matter of fact, several ladies had 'stood' for this series, but the poet had artfully generalised them into one supreme Madonna, whom Annette believed to be herself. Indeed, she had furnished the warmest and the most tragic colouring. Rondel, however, had for some time kept his address a secret from Annette. But the candle set upon a hill cannot be hid : fame has its disadvantages. To a man with creditors or any other form of 'a past,' it is no little dangerous to have his portrait in the *Review of Reviews*. A well-known publisher is an ever-present danger. By some such means Annette had found her poet. The papers could not be decorated with reviews of his verse, and she

not come across some of them. Indeed, she
had, with burning cheek and stormy bosom,
recognised herself in many an intimate confession. It was her hair, her face, all her
beauty, he sang, though the poems were
dedicated to another.

She turned to another passage as she
stood there—'How pretty it sounds *in
poetry*!' she said, and began to read :—

'"There in the odorous meadowsweet afternoon,
    With the lark like the dream of a song in the dreamy
        blue,
    All the air abeat with the wing and buzz of June,
    We met—she and I, I and she," [You and I, I and
        you.]
"And there, while the wild rose and woodbine deliciousness
        blended,
    We kissed and we kissed and we kissed, till the afternoon
        ended. . . ."'

                                                        .

Here Rondel at last interrupted—
'Woman!' he said, 'are your cheeks so
painted that you have lost all sense of
shame?' But she had her answer—
'Man! are you so *great* that you have
lost the sense of pity? And which is the
greater shame : to publish your sins in large
paper and take royalties for them, or to speak
of them, just you and I together, you and

I, as "there in the odorous meadowsweet afternoon"?'

'Look you,' she continued, 'an artist pays his model at least a shilling an hour, and it is only her body he paints: but you use body and soul, and offer her nothing. Your blues and reds are the colours you have stolen from her eyes and her heart—stolen, I say, for the painter pays so much a tube for his colours, so much an hour for his model, but you——' .

'I give you immortality. Poor fly, I give you amber,' modestly suggested the poet.

But Annette repeated the word 'Immortality!' with a scorn that almost shook the poet's conceit, and thereupon produced an account, which ran as follows :—

'Mr. Hyacinth Rondel
Dr. to Miss Annette Jones,
For moiety of the following royalties :—

Moonshine and Meadowsweet, .	500	copies.
Coral and Bells, ...	750	„
Liber Amoris, 3 editions, . .	3,000	„
Forbidden Fruit, 5 editions, .	5,000	„

9,250 copies at 1s.
= £462, 10s.
Moiety of same due to Miss Jones, £231 5s.'

'I don't mind receipting it for two hundred and thirty,' she said, as she handed it to him.

Hyacinth was completely awakened by this: the joke was growing serious. So he at once roused up the bully in him, and ordered her out of his rooms. But she smiled at his threats, and still held out her account. At last he tried coaxing: he even had the insolence to beg her, by the memory of the past they had shared together, to spare him. He assured her that she had vastly overrated his profits, that fame meant far more cry than wool: that, in short, he was up to the neck in difficulties as it was, and really had nothing like that sum in his possession.

'Very well, then,' she replied at last, 'you must marry me instead. Either the money or the marriage. Personally, I prefer the money'—Rondel's egoism twinged like a hollow tooth—'and if you think you can escape me and do neither, look at this!' and she drew a revolver from her pocket.

'They are all loaded,' she added. 'Now, which is it to be?'

Rondel made a movement as if to snatch

the weapon from her, but she sprang back and pointed it at his head.

'If you move, I fire.'

Now one would not need to be a minor poet to be a coward under such circumstances. Rondel could see that Annette meant what she said. She was clearly a desperate woman, with no great passion for life. To shoot him and then herself would be a little thing in the present state of her feelings. Like most poets, he was a prudent man—he hesitated, leaning with closed fist upon the table. She stood firm.

'Come,' she said at length, 'which is it to be—the revolver, marriage, or the money?' She ominously clicked the trigger, 'I give you five minutes.'

It was five minutes to eleven. The clock ticked on while the two still stood in their absurdly tragic attitudes—he still hesitating, she with her pistol in line with the brain that laid the golden verse. The clock whirred before striking the hour. Annette made a determined movement. Hyacinth looked up, he saw she meant it, all the more for the mocking indifference of her expression.

'Once more—death, marriage, or the money?'

The clock struck.

'The money,' gasped the poet.

*   *   *   *   *

But Annette still kept her weapon in line.

'Your cheque-book!' she said. Rondel obeyed.

'Pay Miss Annette Jones, or order, the sum of two hundred and thirty pounds. No, don't cross it!'

Rondel obeyed.

'Now, toss it over to me. You observe I still hold the pistol.'

Rondel once more obeyed. Then, still keeping him under cover of the ugly-looking tube, she backed towards the door.

'Good-bye,' she said. 'Be sure I shall look out for your next volume.'

Rondel, bewildered as one who had lived through a fairy-tale, sank into his chair. Did such ridiculous things happen? He turned to his cheque-book. Yes, there was the counterfoil, fresh as a new wound, from which indeed his bank account was profusely bleeding.

Then he turned to his laurels : but, behold, they were all withered.

So, after a while, he donned hat and coat, and went forth to seek a flatterer as a pick-me-up.

GOOD BISHOP VALENTINE

THE reader will remember how Lamb imagines him as a rubicund priest of Hymen, and pictures him 'attended with thousands and ten thousands of little loves, and the air is

"Brush'd with the hiss of rustling wings."

Singing Cupids are thy choristers and thy precentors ; and instead of the crozier, the mystical arrow is borne before thee.' Alas, who indeed would have expected the bitter historical truth, and have dreamed that poor Valentine, instead of being that rosy vision, was one of the Church's most unhappy martyrs ? Tradition has but two pieces of information about him : that during the reign of Claudius II., probably in the year 270, he was 'first beaten with heavy clubs, and then beheaded' ; and likewise that he was a man of exceptional chastity of character—a fact

46

that may be considered no less paradoxical in regard to his genial reputation. He was certainly the last man to have been the patron saint of young blood, and if he has any cognisance of the frivolities done in his name, the knowledge must be more painful to him than all the clubs of Claudius. Unhappy saint! To have his good name murdered also! To be, through all time, the high-priest of that very 'paganism' which he died to repudiate: the one most potent survival throughout Christian times of the joyous old order he would fain supplant! Could anything be more characteristic of the whimsical humour of Time, which loves nothing better than to make a laughing-stock of human symbolism? The savage putting a stray dress-coat to solemn sacerdotal usage, or taking some blackguard of a Mulvaney for a very god, is not more absurd than mankind thus ignorantly bringing to this poor martyr throughout the years the very last offering he can have desired. Surely it must have filled his shade with a strange bewilderment to have watched us year by year bringing him garlands and the sweet incense of young love, to have seen this gay company approach his shrine with laughter and roses, a very bacchanal, where he had looked for sympathetic sackcloth and ashes —surely it must have all seemed a silly sacrilegious jest. However, he is long since slandered beyond all hope of restitution. So long as the spring moves in the blood, lovers will doubtless continue to take his name in vain, and feign his saintly sanction for their charming indiscretions. Indeed, he is fabled by the poets to be responsible for the billing and cooing of the whole creation. Everybody knows that the birds, too, pair on St. Valentine's Day. We have many a poet's word for it. Donne's charming lines, for instance :

> 'All the air is thy diocese,
> And all the chirping choristers
> And other birds are thy parishioners :
> Thou marriest every year
> The lyrique lark, and the grave whispering dove,
> The sparrow, that neglects his life for love,
> The household bird with the red stomacher ;
> Thou mak'st the blackbird speed as soon
> As doth the goldfinch or the halcyon.'

In fact, it would appear that St. Valentine was, literally, a hedge-priest.

But do lovers, one wonders, still observe his ancient, though mistaken, rites? Do they still have a care whose pretty face they should first set eyes upon on Valentine's morning, like Mistress Pepys, who kept her eyes closed the whole forenoon lest they should portend a *mésalliance* with one of those tiresome 'paynters' at work on the gilding of the pictures and the chimney-piece? Or do they with throbbing hearts 'draw' for the fateful name, or, weighting little inscribed slips of paper with lead or breadcrumbs, and dropping them into a basin of water, breathlessly await the name that shall first float up to the surface? Do they still perform that terrible feat of digestion, which consisted of eating a hard-boiled egg, shell and all, to inspire the presaging dream, and pin five bay-leaves upon their pillows to make it the surer?

We are told they do, these happy super-stitious lovers, though probably the practices obtain now mostly among a class of fair maids who have none of Mrs. Pepys' fears of 'paynters,' and who are not averse even from a bright young plumber. Indeed, it is **to**

be feared that the one sturdy survival of St.
Valentine is to be sought in the 'ugly valentine.' This is another of Time's jests : to
degrade the beautiful and distinguished, and
mock at old-time sanctities with coarse
burlesque. We see it constantly in the
fortunes of old streets and squares, once
graced with the beau and the sedan-chair,
the very cynosure of the polite and elegant
world, but now vocal with the clamorous
wrongs of the charwoman and the melancholy
appeal of the coster. We see it, too, in the
ups and downs of words once aristocratic or
tender, words once the very signet of polite
conversation, now tossed about amid the very
offal of language. We see it when some
noble house, an illustrious symbol of heroic
honour, the ark of high traditions, finds its
reductio ad absurdum in some hare-brained
turf-lord, who defiles its memories as he sells
its pictures. But no lapse could be more
pitiful than the end of St. Valentine. Once
the day on which great gentlemen and great
ladies exchanged stately and, as Pepys
frequently complained, costly compliments ;
when the ingenuity of love tortured itself for

the sweetest conceit wherein to express the
very sweetest thing; the May-day of the
heart, when the very birds were Cupid's
messengers, and all the world wore ribbons
and made pretty speeches. What is it now?
The festival of the servants' hall. It is the
sacred day set apart for the cook to tell the
housemaid, in vividly illustrated verse, that
she need have no fear of the policeman
thinking twice of *her*; for the housemaid to
make ungenerous reflections on 'cookey's'
complexion and weight, and to assure that
'queen of the larder' that it is not her, but
her puddings, that attract the constabulary
heart. It is the day when inoffensive little
tailors receive anonymous letters beginning
'You silly snip,' when the baker is unplea-
santly reminded of his immemorial *sobriquet*
of 'Daddy Dough,' and coarse insult breaks
the bricklayer's manly heart. Perhaps
of all its symbols the most typical and
popular are: a nursemaid, a perambulator
enclosing twins, and a gigantic dragoon.
In fact, we are faced by this curious development—that the day once sacred to
universal compliment is now mainly dedi-

cated to low and foolish insult. Oh, that
whirligig !

Do true lovers still remember the day to
keep it holy, one wonders ? Does Ophelia
still sing beneath the window, and do the
love-birds still carry on their celestial post-
age ? One fears that all have gone with the
sedan-chair, the stage-coach, and last year's
snow. Will the true lovers go next ? But,
indeed, a florist told us that he had sold
many flowers for 'valentines' this year, and
that the prettier practice of sending flowers
was, he thought, supplanting the tawdry and
stereotyped offering of cards. Which reminds
one of an old verse :

> ' The violet made haste to appear,
>   To be her bosom guest,
> With first primrose that grew this year
>   I purchas'd from her breast ;
>   To me,   ·
>   Gave she,
>   Her golden lock for mine ;
>   My ring of jet
>   For her bracelet,
>   I gave my *Valentine.*'

IRRELEVANT PEOPLE

THERE are numberless people who are, doubtless, of much interest and charm—in their proper context. That context we feel, however, is not our society. We have no objection to their carrying on the business of human beings, so long as they allow us an uninterrupted trading of, say, a hundred miles. Within that charmed and charming circle they should not set foot, and we are quite willing in addition, for them, to gird themselves about with the circumference of another thousand. It is not that they are disagreeable or stupid, or in any way obviously objectionable. Bores are more frequently clever than dull, and the only all-round definition of a bore is—The Person We Don't Want. Few people are bores at all times and places, and indeed one might venture on the charitable axiom: that when people bore us we are pretty sure to be boring them at the same time. The bore, to attempt a further definition, is simply a fellow human being out of his element. It is said by travellers from distant lands that fishes will not live out of water. It is a no less familiar fact that certain dull metals need to be placed in oxygen to show off their brilliant parts. So is it with the bore : set him in the oxygen of his native admiration, and he will scintillate like a human St. Catherine wheel, though in your society he was not even a Chinese cracker. Every man needs his own stage and his own audience.

> ' Hath not love
> Made for all these their sweet particular air
> To shine in, their own beams and names to bear,
> Their ways to wander and their wards to keep,
> Till story and song and glory and all things sleep.'

Mr. Swinburne asked the question of lovers, but perhaps it is none the less applicable to the bore or irrelevant person. Yet a third definition of the latter here suggests itself. To be born for each other is, obviously, to be lovers. Well, not to be born for each

other is to be bores. In future, let us not
speak unkindly of the tame bore, let us say
—'We were not born for each other.'

Relations do not, perhaps, invariably
suggest the first line of 'Endymion'; indeed, they are, one fears, but infrequently
celebrated in song. But the same word in
the singular, how beautiful it is! Relation!
In that little word is the whole secret of life.
To get oneself placed in perfect harmony of
relation with the world around us, to have
nothing in our lives that we wouldn't buy,
to possess nothing that is not sensitive to
us, ready to ring a fairy chime of association
at our slightest touch: no irrelevant book,
picture, acquaintance, or activity—ah me!
you may well say it is an ideal. Yes, it is
what men have meant by El Dorado, The
Promised Land, and all such shy haunts of
the Beatific Vision. Probably the quest of
the Philosopher's Stone is not more wild.
Yet men still seek that precious substitute
for Midas. Brave spirits! Unconquerable
idealists! Salt of the earth!

But if it be admitted that the quest of the
Perfect Relation (in two senses) is hopeless,

yet there is no reason why we should not approach as near to it as we can.

We can at least begin by barring the irrelevant person—in other words, choosing our own acquaintance. Of course, we have no entire free-will in so important a matter. Free-will is like the proverbial policeman, never there when most wanted. There are two classes of more or less irrelevant persons that cannot be entirely avoided : our blood-relations, and our business-relations —both often so pathetically distinct from our heart-relations and our brain-relations. Well, our business-relations need not trouble us over much. They are not, as the vermin-killer advertisement has it, 'pests of the household.' They come out only during business hours. The curse of the blood-relation, however, is that he infests your leisure moments ; and you must notice the pathos of that verbal distinction : man measures his toil by 'hours' (office-hours), his leisure by 'moments !'

But let not the reader mistake me for a Nero. The claims of a certain degree of blood-relationship I not only admit, but welcome as a sacred joy. Their experience is unhappy for whom the bonds of parentage, of sisterhood and brotherhood, will not always have a sort of involuntary religion. If a man should not exactly be tied to his mother's apron-string, he should all his life remain tied to her by that other mysterious cord which no knife can sever. Uncles and aunts may, under certain circumstances, be regarded as sacred, and meet for occasional burnt-offerings; but beyond them I hold that the knot of blood-relationship may be regarded as Gordian, and ruthlessly cut. Cousins have no claims. Indeed, the scale of the legacy duties, like few legalities, follows the natural law. The further removed, the greater tax should our blood-relations pay for our love, or our legacy; but the heart-relation, the brain-relation ('the stranger in blood'), he alone should go untaxed altogether! Alas, the Inland Revenue Commissioners would charge him more than any, which shows that their above-mentioned touch of nature was but a fluke, after all.

It is impossible to classify the multitude of remaining irrelevancies, who, were

one to permit them, would fall upon our
leisure like locusts ; but possibly 'friends
of the family,' 'friends from the country,'
and 'casuals' would include the most
able-bodied. Sentiment apart, old school-
fellows should, if possible, be avoided ; and
no one who merely knew us when we were
babies (really a very limited elementary
acquaintance) and has mistaken us ever
since should be admitted within the gates—
though we might introduce him to our own
baby as the nearest match.   The child is not
father to the man.   It was a merely verbal
paradox, which shows Wordsworth's ignorance of humanity.   Let me especially warn
the reader, particularly the newly-married
reader, against the type of friend from the
country who, so soon as they learn you have
set up house in London, suddenly discovers
an interest in your fortunes which, like
certain rivers, has run underground further
than you can remember.   They write and
tell you that they are thinking of coming to
town, and would like to spend a few days
with you.   They leave their London address
vague.   It has the look of a blank which you

are expected to fill up. You shrewdly sur-
mise that, so to say, they meditate paying a
visit to Euston, and spending a fortnight
with you on the way. But if you are wise
and subtle and strong, you cut this acquaintance ruthlessly, as you lop a branch. Such
are the dead wood of your life. Cut it away
and cast it into the oven of oblivion. Don't
fear to hurt it. These people care as little
for you, as you for them. All they want is
board and lodging, and if you give in to
them, you may be an amateur hotel-keeper
all your days.

Another 'word to the newly-married.' Be
not over-solicitous of wedding-presents.
They carry a terrible rate of interest. A
silver toast-rack will never leave you a Bank
Holiday secure, and a breakfast service
means at least a fortnight's 'change' to one
or more irrelevant persons twice a year.
They have been known to stay a month
on the strength of an egg-boiler. So, be
warned, I pray you. Wedding-presents are
but a form of loan, which you are expected
to pay back, with compound interest at 50
per cent., in 'hospitality,' 'entertainment,'

and your still more precious time. For the
givers of wedding-presents there is no more
profitable form of investment. But you, be
wise, and buy your own.

There is a peculiar joy in snubbing irrelevant would-be country visitors. It is the
sweetest exercise of the will. Especially,
too, if they are conceited persons who made
sure of invitation. It adds a yet deeper
thrill to the pleasure if you are able to invite
some other friends near at hand, of humbler
mind and greater interest, whose (maybe)
shy charms are not flauntingly revealed.
'Fancy So-and-So being invited ! I shouldn't
have thought they had anything in common.'
How sweet is the imagination of that
wounded whisper. It makes you feel like a
(German) prince. You have the power of
making happy and (even better in some
cases) unhappy, at least, as Carlyle would
say, 'to the extent of sixpence.'

You have tasted the sweets of choosing
your own friends, and snubbing the others.
You have gone so far towards the attainment
of the harmonious environment, the Perfect
Relation. Your friends shall be as carefully

selected, shall mean as much to you as your books and flowers and pictures; and your leisure shall be a priest's garden, in which none but the chosen may walk.

Yet, in spite of my little burst of Neroics, I am far from advising a cruel treatment of the Irrelevant Person. Let us not forget what we said at the beginning, that he is probably an interesting person in the wrong place. He has taken the wrong turning— into your company. Do unto him as you would he might do unto you. Direct him aright—that is to say, out of it! Remember, we are all bores in certain uncongenial social climates: all stars in our own particular milky way. So, remember, don't be cruel—as a rule—to the Irrelevant Person; but just smile your best at him, and whisper : ' We were not born for each other.'

THE DEVILS ON THE NEEDLE

... ' these things are life :
And life, some say, is worthy of the muse.'

I

THERE is a famous query of the old school-
man at which we have all flung a jest in our
time : *How many angels can dance on the
point of a needle?* In a world with so many
real troubles it seems, perhaps, a little idle
to worry too long over the question. Yet
in the mere question, putting any answer
outside possibility, there is a wonderful
suggestiveness, if it has happened to come
to you illuminated by experience. It becomes a little clearer, perhaps, if we substitute devils for angels. A friend of mine
used always to look at it thus inversely
when he quarrelled with his wife. Forgive
so many enigmas to start with, but it was

this way. They never quarrelled more than three times a year, and it was always on the very smallest trifle, one particular trifle too. On the great things of life they were at one. It was but a tiny point, a needle's end of difference, on which they disagreed, and it was on that needle's end that the devils danced. All the devils of hell, you would have said. At any rate, you would have no longer wondered why the old philosopher put so odd a question, for you had only to see little Dora's face lit up with fury over that ridiculous trifle to have exclaimed : ' Is it possible that so many devils can dance on a point where there seems hardly footing for a frown ? '

However, so it was, and when I tell you what the needle's end was, you will probably not think me worth a serious person's attention. That I shall, of course, regret, but it was simply this : Dora *would* write with a ' J ' pen—for which it was William's idiosyncrasy to have an unconquerable aversion. She might, you will think, have given way to her husband on so absurd a point, a mere pen-point of disagreement.

He was the tenderest of husbands in every
other point. There is nothing that love
can dream that he was not capable of
doing for his wife's sake. But, on the
other hand, it was equally true that there
can be no other wife in the world more
devoted than Dora ; with her also there
was nothing too hard for love's sake. Could
he not waive so ridiculous a blemish ? It
was little enough for love to achieve,
surely. Yes, strange as it seems, their love
was equal to impossible heroisms : to have
died for each other had been easy, but to
surrender this pen-point was impossible.
And, alas ! as they always do, the devils
found out this needle's end—and danced.
For their purpose it was as good as a plat-
form. It gave them joy indeed to think
what stupendous powers of devilry they
could concentrate on so tiny a stage.

It was a sad thing, too, that Dora and
William were able to avoid the subject three
hundred and sixty-four days of the year, but
on that odd day it was sure to crop up.
Perhaps they had been out late the night
before, and their nerves were against them.

The merest accident would bring it on. Dora would ask William to post a letter for her in town. Being out of sorts and susceptible to the silliest irritation, he would not be able to resist criticising the addressing. If he didn't mention it, Dora would notice his 'expression.' That would be 'quite enough,' you may be sure. Half the tragedies of life depend on 'expression.'

'Well!' she would say.

'Well what?' he would answer, already beginning to tremble.

'You have one of your critical moods on again.'

'Not at all. What's the matter?'

'You have, I say. . . . Well, why do you look at the envelope in that way? I know what it is, well enough.'

'If you know, dear, why do you ask?'

'Don't try to be sarcastic, dear. It is so vulgar.'

'I hadn't the least intention of being so.'

'Yes, you had. . . . Give me that letter.'

'All right.'

'Yes, you admire every woman's writing but your wife's.'

E

'Don't be silly, dear. See, I don't feel
very well this morning. I don't want to be
angry.'

'Angry! Be angry; what does it matter
to me? Be as angry as you like. I wish I
had never seen you.'

'Somewhat of a *non sequitur*, is it not, my.
love?'

'Don't "my love" me. With your nasty
cool sarcasm!'

'Isn't it better to try and keep cool rather
than to fly into a temper about nothing?
See, I know you are a little nervous this
morning. Let us be friends before I go.'

'I have no wish to be friends.'

'Dora!'

William would then lace his boots, and
don his coat in silence, before making a final
effort at reconciliation.

'Well, dear, good-bye. Perhaps you will
love me again by the time I get home.'

'Perhaps I shan't be here when you come
home.'

'For pity's sake, don't begin that silly
nonsense, Dora.'

'It isn't silly nonsense. I say again—I

mayn't be here when you come home, and I mean it.'

'Oh, all right then. Suppose I were to say that I won't come home?'

'I should be quite indifferent.'

'Oh, Dora!'

'I would. I am weary of our continual quarrels. I can bear this life no longer.' (It was actually sunny as a summer sky.)

'Why, it was only last night you said how happy we were.'

'Yes, but I didn't mean it.'

'Didn't mean it! Don't talk like that, or I shall lose myself completely.'

'You will lose your train if you don't mind. Don't you think you had better go?'

'Can you really talk to me like that?— me?—Oh, Dora, it is not you that is talking: it is some devil in you.'

Then suddenly irritated beyond all control by her silly little set face, he would blurt out a sudden, 'Oh, very well, then!' and before she was aware of it, the door would have banged. By the time William had reached the gate he would be half-way through with a deed of assignment in favour of his wife,

who, now that he had really gone, would
watch him covertly from the window with
slowly thawing heart.

So the devils would begin their dance:
for it was by no means ended. Of course,
William would come home as usual; and
yet, though the sound of his footstep was
the one sound she had listened for all day,
Dora would immediately begin to petrify
again, and when he would approach her
with open arms, asking her to forgive and
forget the morning, she would demur just
long enough to set him alight again. Heaven,
how the devils would dance then! And the
night would usually end with them lying
sleepless in distant beds.

II

To attempt tragedy out of such absurd
material is, you will say, merely stupid.
Well, I'm sorry. I know no other way to
make it save life's own, and I know that the
tragedy of William's life hung upon a silly
little ink-stained 'J' pen. I would pretend
that it was made of much more grandiose
material if I could. But the facts are as I

shall tell you. And surely if you fulfil that definition of man which describes him as a reflective being, if you ever think on life at all, you must have noticed how even the great tragedies that go in purple in the great poets all turn on things no less trifling in themselves, all come of people pretending to care for some bauble more than they really do.

And you must have wondered, too, as you stood awestruck before the regal magnificence, the radiant power, the unearthly beauty, of those glorious and terrible angels of passion—that splendid creature of wrath, that sorrow wonderful as a starlit sky—you must have wondered that life has not given these noble elementals material worthier of their fiery operation than the paltry concerns of humanity ; just as you may have wondered too, that so god-like a thing as fire should find nothing worthier of its divine fury than the ugly accumulations of man.

At any rate, I know that all the sorrow that saddens, sanctifies, and sometimes terrifies my friend, centres round that silly little 'J' pen. The difference is that the angels dance on its point now, instead of the devils ; but it is too late.

A night of unhappiness had ended once more as I described. The long darkness had slowly passed, and morning, sunny with forgiveness, had come at length. William's heart yearned for his wife in the singing of the birds. He would first slip down into the garden and gather her some fresh flowers, then steal with them into the room and kiss her little sulky mouth till she awoke ; and, before she remembered their sorrow, her eyes would see the flowers.

It was a lover's simple thought, sweeter even than the flowers he had soon gathered.

But, then, reader, why tease you with transparent secrets ? You know that Dora could not smell the flowers.

You know that Death had come to dance with the devils that night, and that Dora and William would quarrel about little 'J' pens no more for ever.

POETS AND PUBLISHERS

I

A SERIOUS theme demands serious treatment. Let us, therefore, begin with definitions. What is a poet? and what is a
publisher? Popularly speaking, a poet is a
fool, and a publisher is a knave. At least,
I am hardly wrong in saying that such is
the literal assumption of the Incorporated
Society of Authors, a body well acquainted
with both. Indeed, that may be said to be
its working hypothesis, the very postulate
of its existence.

Of course, there are other definitions of
both. It is not so the maiden of seventeen
defines a poet, as she looks up to him with
brimming eyes in the summer sunset and
calls him 'her Byron.' It is not so the
embryo Chatterton defines him, chained to
an office stool in some sooty provincial

town, dreaming of Fleet Street as of a
shining thoroughfare in the New Jerusalem,
where move authors and poets, angelic
beings, in 'solemn troops and sweet socie-
ties.' For, indeed, was that not the dream
of all of us? For my part, I remember my
first, most beautiful, delusion, was that poets
belonged only to the golden prime of
the world, and that, like miracles, they had
long ceased before the present age. And I
very well recall my curious bewilderment
when, one day in a bookseller's, a friendly
schoolmaster took up a new volume of Mr.
Swinburne's and told me that it was by the
new great poet. How wonderful that little
incident made the world for me! Real
poets actually existing in this unromantic
to-day! If you had told me of a mermaid,
or a wood-nymph, or of the philosopher's
stone as apprehensible wonders, I should
not have marvelled more. While a single
poet existed in the land, who could say
that the kingdom of Romance was all let
out in building lots, or that the steam
whistle had quite 'frighted away the Dryads
and the Fauns.'

Since then I have taken up the reviewing of minor verse as a part of my livelihood, and where I once saw the New Jerusalem I see now the New Journalism.

There are, doubtless, many who still cherish that boyish dream of the poet. He still stalks through the popular imagination with his Spanish hat and cloak, his amaranthine locks, his finely-frenzied eyes, and his Alastor-like forgetfulness of his meals. But only, it is to be feared, for a little time. For the latter-day poet is doing his best to dissipate that venerable tradition. Bitten by the modern passion for uniformity, he has French-cropped those locks, in which, as truly as with Samson, lay his strength, he has discarded his sombrero for a Lincoln and Bennett, he cultivates a silky moustache, a glossy boot, and has generally given himself into the hands of the West-End tailor. Stung beyond endurance by taunts of his unpracticality, he enters Parliament, edits papers, keeps accounts, and is in every way a better business man than his publisher.

This is all very well for a little time. The contrast amuses by its piquancy. To write

of wild and whirling things in your books,
but in public life to be associated with
nothing more wild and whirling than a
shirt-fronted eye-glassed hansom; to be
at heart an Alastor, but in appearance a
bank-clerk, delights an age of paradox.

But, though it may pay for a while, it
will, I am sure, prove a disastrous policy
in the long run. The poet unborn shall, I
am certain, rue it. The next generation of
poets (or, indeed, writers generally) will reap
a sorrowful harvest from the gratuitous dis-
illusionment, with which the present generation is so eager to indulge the curiosity, and
flatter the mediocrity, of the public. The
public, like the big baby it is, is continually
crying 'to see the wheels go round,' and for
a time the exhibition of, so to say, the
'works' of poet and novelist is profitable.
But a time will come when, with its curiosity
sated, the public will turn upon the poet,
and throw into his face, on his own authority,
that he is but as they are, that his airs of
inspiration and divine right are humbug.
And in that day the poet will block his silk
hat, will shave away the silken moustache,

will get him a bottle of Mrs. Allen's Hair
Restorer, and betake himself to the sombrero
of his ancestors—but it will be all too late.
The cat will have been irrecoverably let out
of the bag, the mystery of the poet as
exploded as the mysteries of Eleusis.

Tennyson knew better. To use the word
in its mediæval sense, he respected the
'mystery' of poetry. Instinctively, doubtless, but also, I should imagine, deliberately,
he all his life lived up to the traditional
type of the poet, and kept between him and
his public a proper veil of Sinaitic mist.
You remember Browning's picture of the
mysterious poet 'you saw go up and down
Valladolid,' and the awestruck rumours
that were whispered about him—how, for
instance—

> ' If you tracked him to his home, down lanes
> Beyond the Jewry, and as clean to pace,
> You found he ate his supper in a room
> Blazing with lights, four Titians on the wall,
> And twenty naked girls to change his plate ! '

That is the kind of thing the public likes to
hear of its poets. That is something like
a poet. Inquisitive the public always will
be, but it is a mistake to indulge rather

than to pique its curiosity. Tennyson
respected the wishes of his public in this
matter, and, not only in his dress and his
dramatic seclusion, but surely in his obstin-
ate avoidance of prose-work of any kind
we have a subtler expression of his careful-
ness for fame. It is a mistake for a poet
to write prose, however good, for it is a
charming illusion of the public that, com-
paratively speaking, any one can write prose.
It is an earthly accomplishment, it is as
walking is to flying—is it not stigmatised
'pedestrian?' Now, your true Bird of
Paradise, which is the poet, must, metaphorically speaking, have no legs — as
Adrian Harley said was the case with
the women in Richard Feverel's poems.
He must never be seen to walk in prose,
for his part is, 'pinnacled dim in the
intense inane,' to hang aloft and warble the
unpremeditated lay, without erasure or blot.
This is, I am sure, not fanciful, for two or
three modern instances, which I am far too
considerate to name, illustrate its truth.
Unless you are a very great person indeed,
the surest way to lose a reputation as poet

is to gain one as critic. It is true that for a time one may help the other, and that if you are very fecund, and let your poetical issues keep pace with your critical, you may even avoid the catastrophe altogether; but it is an unmistakable risk, and if in the end you are not catalogued as a great critic, you will assuredly be set down as a minor poet: whereas if you had stuck to your last, there is no telling what fame might not have been yours. Limitation, not versatility, is the fashion to-day. The man with the one talent, not the five, is the hero of the hour.

Besides, this sudden change of his spots on the part of the poet is unfair to the publisher, who is thus apt to find himself surprised out of his just gain. For, at the present moment, I would back almost any poet of my acquaintance against any publisher in a matter of business. This is unfair, for the publisher is a being slow to move, slow to take in changed conditions, always two generations, at least, behind his authors. Consequently, this sudden development of capacity on the part of the poet is liable to take him unprepared, and the mere

apparition of a poet who can add up a
pounds shillings and pence column offhand
might well induce apoplexy. Yet it is to be
feared that that providence which arms
every evil thing with its fang, has so pro-
tected the publisher with an instinctive
dread of verse in any form, and especially
in manuscript, that he has, after all, little
to fear from the poet's new gifts.

II

But, indeed, my image just now was both
uncomplimentary and unjust: for, parallel
with the change in the poet to which I have
referred, a still more unnatural change is
making itself apparent in the type of the
publisher. It would almost seem as if the
two are changing places. Instead of the poet
humbly waiting, hat in hand, kicking his
heels for half-a-day in the publisher's office,
it is the publisher who seeks him, who writes
for appointments at his private house, or in-
vites him to dinner. Yet it behoves the poet
to be on his guard. A publisher, like another
personage, has many shapes of beguile-
ment, and it is not unlikely that this flatter-

ing deference is but another wile to entrap the unwary. There is no way of circumventing the dreamer so subtle as to flatter his business qualities. We all like to be praised for the something we cannot do. It is for this reason that Mr. Stevenson interferes with Samoan politics, when he should be writing romances—just the desire of the dreamer to play the man of action.

But I am not going to weary you by indulging in the stale old diatribes against the publisher. For, to speak seriously the honest truth, I think they are in the main a very much abused race. Thackeray put the matter with a good deal of common-sense, in that scene in 'Pendennis,' where Pen and Warrington walk home together from the Fleet prison, after hearing Captain Shandon read that brilliant prospectus of the *Pall Mall Gazette*, which he had written for bookseller Bungay, and for which that gentleman disbursed him a £5 note on the spot. Pen, you will remember, was full of the oppressions of genius, of Apollo being tied down to such an Admetus as Bungay Warrington, however, took a maturer view of the matter.

'A fiddlestick about men of genius!' he
exclaimed, 'I deny that there are so many
geniuses as people who whimper about the
fate of men of letters assert there are. There
are thousands of clever fellows in the world
who could, if they would, turn verses, write
articles, read books, and deliver a judgment
upon them ; the talk of professional critics
and writers is not a whit more brilliant, or
profound, or amusing than that of any other
society of educated people. If a lawyer, or a
soldier, or a parson outruns his income, and
does not pay his bills, he must go to gaol ;
and an author must go too. If an author
fuddles himself, I don't know why he should
be let off a headache the next morning—if
he orders a coat from the tailor's, why he
shouldn't pay for it. . . .'

Dr. Johnson, who had no great reason
to be prejudiced in their favour, defined
booksellers as 'the patrons of literature,' and
M. Anatole France has recently said that 'a
great publisher is a kind of Minister for *belles-
lettres.*' Such definitions are, doubtless, pro-
phecies of the ideal rather than descriptions of
the actual. Yet, fairly dealt with, the history

of publishing would show a much nearer living up to them on the part of publishers than the poets and their sentimental sympathisers are inclined to admit. We hear a great deal of Milton getting £10 for *Paradise Lost*, and the Tonsons riding in their carriage, but seldom of Cottle adventuring thirty guineas on Coleridge's early poems, or the Jacksons giving untried boys £10—or, according to some accounts, £20—for *Poems by Two Brothers*.

To open the case for the bookseller or the publisher. The poet, to start with, bases his familiar complaints on a wilful disregard of the relation which poetry bears to average humanity. You often hear him express indignant surprise that the sale of butcher's meat should be a more lucrative business than the sale of poetry. But, surely, to argue thus is to manifest a most absurd misapprehension of the facts of life. Wordsworth says that 'we live by admiration, joy, and love.' So doubtless we do: but we live far more by butcher's meat and Burton ale. Poetry is but a preparation of opium distilled by a minority for a minority. The poet may test

F

the case by the relative amounts he pays his butcher and his bookseller. So far as I know, he pays as little for his poetry as possible, and never buys a volume by a brother-singer till he has vainly tried six different ways to get a presentation copy. The poet seems incapable of mastering the rudimentary truth that ethereals must be based on materials. 'No song, no supper' is the old saw. It is equally true reversed—no supper, no song. The empty-stomach theory of creation is a cruel fallacy, though undoubtedly hunger has sometimes been the spur which the clear soul doth raise.

The conditions of existence compel the publisher to be a tradesman on the same material basis as any other. Ideally, a poem, like any other beautiful thing, is beyond price ; but, practically, its value depends on the number of individuals who can be prevailed upon to purchase it. In its ethereal —otherwise its unprinted—state, it is only subject to the laws of the celestial ether, one of which is that it yields no money ; properly speaking, money is there an irrelevant condition. Byron, you remember, would not for a long time accept any money from Murray for his poems, successful as they were. He had a proper sense of the indignity of *selling* the children of his soul. The incongruity is much as though we might go to Portland Road and buy an angel, just as we buy a parrot. The transactions of poetry and of sale are on two different planes. But so soon as, shall we say, you debase poetry by bringing it down to the lower plane, it becomes subject to the laws of that plane. An un-printed poem is a spiritual thing, but a printed poem is subject to the laws of matter. In the heaven of the poet's imagination there are no printers and paper-makers, no binders, no discounts to the trade and thirteen to the dozen ; but on earth, where alone, so far as we know, books exist, these terrestrial beings and conditions are of paramount importance, and cannot be ignored. It may be perfectly true that a certain poem is so fine that, in a properly constituted cosmogony, it ought to support you to the end of your days ; but is the publisher to blame because, in spite of its manifest genius, he can sell no more than 500 copies ?

Then, to take another point of view, it is, I think, quite demonstrable that, compared with the men of many other callings, a poet who can get his verses accepted is very well paid. Take a typical instance. You spend an absolutely beatific evening with Clarinda in the moonlit woodland. You go home and relieve your emotions in a sonnet, which, we will say, at a generous allowance, takes you half-an-hour to write. Next morning in that cold calculating mood for which no business man can match a poet, you copy it out fair and send it to a friendly editor. Perhaps out of Clarinda alone you beget a sonnet a week, which at £2, 2s. a week is £109, 4s. a year—not to speak of Phyllis and Dulcinea. At any rate, take that one sonnet. For an evening with Clarinda, for which alone you would have paid the sum, and for a beggarly half-hour's work, you receive as much as many a City clerk earns by six hard days' work, eight hours to the dreary day, with perhaps a family to keep and a railway contract to pay for. Half-an-hour's work, and if you can live on £2, 2s. a week, the rest of your time is free as air! Moreover, you have the option of going about with a feeling that you are a being vastly superior to your fellows, because forsooth you can string fourteen lines together in decent Petrarcan form, and they cannot. And to return for a moment to Clarinda: it seems to me that your publisher, with all his ill-gotten gains, compares favourably with you in your treatment of your partner in the production of that sonnet. What about the woman's half-profits in the matter? For, remember, if the publisher depends on the brains of the poet, the poet is no less dependent on the heart of the woman. It is from woman, in nine cases out of ten, that the poets have drawn their inspiration. And how have they, in eight cases out of this nine, treated her? The story is but too familiar. Will it always seem so much worse to pick a man's brains than to break a woman's heart?

We touched just now on the arrogance of the poet. It is one of the most foolish and distasteful of his faults, and one which unfortunately the world has conspired from time immemorial to confirm. He has been too long the spoiled child, too long allowed to

think that anything becomes him, too long
allowed to ride rough-shod over the neck or
the average man.

Mrs. Browning, in *Aurora Leigh*, while
celebrating the poet, sneers at 'your common
men' who 'lay telegraphs, gauge railroads,
reign, reap, dine.' But why? All these—
with, perhaps, the exception of reigning—
are very proper and necessary things to be
done, and any one of them, done in the
true spirit of work, is every bit as dignified
as the writing of poetry, and often, I am
afraid, a great deal more so. This scorn of
the common man is but another instance of
the poet's ignorance of the facts of life and
the relations of things. The hysterical bitter-
ness with which certain sections of modern
people of taste are constantly girding at the
bourgeois—which, indeed, as Omar Khayyám
says, heeds 'As the sea's self should heed a
pebble-cast'—is one of the most melancholy
of recent literary phenomena. It was not
so the great masters treated the common
man, nor any full-blooded age. But the
torch of taste has for the moment fallen into
the hands of little men, anæmic and atra-

bilious, with neither laughter nor pity in their hearts.

Besides, how easy it is to misjudge your so-called 'common man.' That fat undistinguished-looking Briton in the corner of the omnibus is as likely as not Mr. So-and-So, the distinguished poet; and who but those with the divining-rod of a kind heart know what refined sensibility and nobility of character may lurk under an extremely *bourgeois* exterior?

We live in an age of every man his own priest and his own lawyer. At a pinch we can very well be every man his own poet. If the whole supercilious crew of modern men of letters, artists, and critics were wiped off the earth to-morrow, the world would be hardly conscious of the loss. Nay, if even the entire artistic accumulation of the past were to be suddenly swallowed up, it would be little worse off. For the world is more beautiful and wonderful than anything that has ever been written about it, and the most glorious picture is not so beautiful as the face of a spring morning.

APOLLO'S MARKET

THE question is sometimes asked—'How poets sell?' One feels inclined idealistically to ask, 'Ought poets to sell?' What can poets want with money?—dear children of the rainbow, who from time immemorial

> . . . on honeydew have fed
> And drunk the milk of Paradise.

Have you never felt a sort of absurdity in paying for a rose—especially if you paid in copper? To pay for a thing of beauty in coin of extreme ugliness! There is obviously no equality of exchange in the transaction. In fact, it is little short of an insult to the flower-girl to pretend that you thus satisfy the obligation. Far better let her give it you—for the love of beauty—as very likely, if you explained the incongruity, she would be glad to do: for flower-girls, no doubt, like

88

every one else, can only have chosen their
particular profession because of its being a
joy for ever. There might be fitness in
offering a kiss on account, though that, of
course, would depend on the flower-girl. To
buy other things with flowers were not so
incongruous. I have often thought of trying
my tobacconist with a tulip; and certainly
an orchid—no very rare one either—should
cover one's household expenses for a week,
if not a fortnight.

Omar Khayyám used to wonder what
the vintners buy 'one half so precious as
the stuff they sell.' It is surely natural to
wonder in like manner of the poet. What
have we to offer in exchange for his priceless manna? One feels that he should be
paid on the mercantile principles of 'Goblin
Market.' Said Laura:—

> 'Good folk, I have no coin;
> To take were to purloin;
> I have no copper in my purse,
> I have no silver either. . . '

Copper! silver even! The goblin-men were
more artistic than that; they realised the

absurdity of paying for immortal things in
coin of mere mortality. So :—

> ' You have much gold upon your head,'
> They answered all together :
> ' Buy from us with a golden curl.'

Yes, those are the ideal rates at which poetry
should be paid. We should, of course, pay
for fairy goods in fairy-gold.

One of the few such appropriate transactions I remember was Queen Elizabeth's
buying a poem from Sir Philip Sidney,
literally, with a lock of her 'gowden hair.'
Poem and lock now lie together at Wilton,
both untouched of time. Or was it that Sir
Philip Sidney paid for the lock with his
poem? However it was, the exchange was
appropriate. The ratio between the thing
sold and the price given was fairly equal.
And, at all times, it is far less absurd for
a poet to pay for the earthly thing with
his poem (thus leaving us to keep the
change), than that we should think to pay
him for his incorruptible with our corruptible.
There would, no doubt, be a subtle element
of absurdity in a poet consenting to pay his

tailor for a suit with a sonnet, while it would obviously be beyond all proportion monstrous for a tailor to think to buy a sonnet with a suit.   Yet a poet might, perhaps, be brought to consider the transaction, if he chanced to be of a gentle disposition.

Yes, the true, the tasteful way to pay a poet is by the exchange of some other beautiful thing : by beautiful praise, by a beautiful smile, by a well-shaped tear, by a rose.   It is thus that a poet—frequently, I am bound to confess — finds his highest reward.

At the same time, there is a subtle ironic pleasure in taking the world's money for poetry—even though one pays it over to a charity immediately—for one feels that the world, for some reason or another, has been persuaded to buy something which it didn't really want, and which it will throw away so soon as we are round the corner.   If the reader has ever published a volume of verse, he must often have chuckled with an unnatural glee over the number of absolutely unpoetic good souls who, from various motives—the

unhappy accident of relationship, perhaps—
have 'subscribed.' Most of us have sound
unpoetic uncles. Of course, you make them
buy you—in large-paper too. Have you ever
gloatingly pictured their absolute bewilderment as, with a stern sense of family pride,
they sit down to cut your pages? Think of
the poor souls thus ' moving about in worlds
not realised.'

A perfect instance of this cruelty to the
Philistine occurs to me. The poet in question is one whose *forte* is children's poetry.
Very tender some of his poems are. You
will find them now and again in *St. Nicholas*,
and he is not unknown in this country.
With a heart like a lamb for children, he
is like a hawk upon the Philistine. I remember an occasion, before he published
a volume, when we were together in a
tavern, in a country-town, a tavern thronged
with farmers on market days. The poet had
some prospectuses in his pocket. Suddenly
a great John Bull would come bumping in
like a cockchafer, and call for his pint. ' Just
you watch,' the poet would say, and away he
crossed over to his victim. ' Good morning,

Mr. Oats!' 'Why, good morning, sir. How-d'ye-do; I hardly know'd thee.' Then presently the voice of the charmer unto the farmer—'Mr. Oats, you care for children, don't you?' 'Ay, ay,' would answer the farmer, a little doubtfully, 'when they're little'uns.' 'Well you know I'm what they, call a poet.' To this Mr. Oats would respond with a good round laugh, as of a man enjoying a good thing. This was very subtle of the poet, for it put the farmer on good terms with himself. He wondered, as he had his laugh over again, how a man could choose to be a poet, when he might have been a farmer. 'Well, I'm bringing out a book of poems all about children—here is one of them!' and the poet would read some humorous thing, such as 'Breeching Tommy.' Then another — such simple pictures of humanity at the age of two, that the farmer could not but be moved to that primary artistic delight, the recognition of the familiar. Then the farmer would grow grave, as he always did at any approach to a purchase, however small, while the poet would rapidly speak of the fitness of the

volume as a present to the old woman:
'Women cared for such things,' he would add
pityingly. Then the farmer would cautiously
ask the price, and blow his cheeks out in
surprise on hearing that it was five shillings.
He had never given so much for a book
in his life. The poet would then insidiously
suggest that by subscribing before publi-
cation he would save a discount. This
would arouse the farmer's instinct for getting
things cheap; and so, finally, with a little
more 'playing,' Mr. Timothy Oats, of Clod
Hall, Salop, was landed high and dry on
the subscription list—a list, by the way,
which already included all the poet's
tradesmen! This is one example of 'how
poets sell.'

Yet over and above what we may term these
forced sales, the demand for verse, we are
assured, is growing. The impression to the
contrary on the part of the Philistine is a
delusion, a false security. And the demand,
a well-known publisher has told us, is an
intelligent one, for poetry of the markedly
idealistic, or markedly realistic, kind: but to
writers of the merely sentimental he can offer

no hope. Their golden age, a pretty long
one while it lasted, has probably gone for
ever.

This is good news for those engaged in
growing dreams for the London market.

THE
'GENIUS' SUPERSTITION

IT must be very painful to the sentimentalist
to notice what common sense is beginning
to prevail on one of his pet subjects : that
of the ancient immunities of 'genius.' Of
course, to a great many good people genius
continues still to be accepted as payment
in full for every species of obligation, and if
a man were a great poet he might probably
still ruin a woman's life, and some, in secret
at least would deem that he did God service.
There are perhaps even more women than
ever nowadays who would, as Keats put it,
like to be married to an epic, and given
away by a three-volume novel. Such an
attitude, however, is more and more taking
its place among the superstitions, and the
divine right of genius to ride rough-shod
over us is at a discount.

At the same time, our national capacity for reaching right conclusions by the wrong course is in this matter once more exemplified. In the main, as usual, our reasoning seems to have been quite astray. We have argued as though for ourselves, and that on those lines we should have reached the same conclusion is somewhat surprising. Because, indeed, it does pay *the world* to allow genius to do its pleasure : its victims even have little to complain of ; they wear the martyr's crown, and if a few tradesmen or a few women are the worse, it has been deemed just, time out of mind, that such should suffer for the people. But the one whom it does not pay, either in this world or the next, is emphatically the man of genius himself. It is really on his behalf that the protest against his ancient immunities should be made, for

'Whether a man serve God or his own whim
Matters not much in the end to any one but him.'

To take the threadbare instance, the world suffered nothing from the suicide of Harriet Westbrook : rather it gained by one more story of tragic pathos. Harriet her-

G

self was no loser, for she had lived her dream, and the stern joy of a great sorrow was granted her to die with : it was only the selfish heart that could leave her thus to suffer and die that was the loser. Not in its relations with the world, fair or ill—such, like all external things, are important only as we take them : but in its diminished capacity to feel greatly and tenderly, in its added numbness, in its less noble beat. It was thus that the *cor cordium* lost what no lyric passion, no triumphant exultation of success, could give to it again.

However, Shelley and his story belong more or less to the tragic muse, and this subject is, perhaps, rather more the property of the comic : for great poets are rare, and really it is the smaller genius we have always with us that is likely to suffer most from those 'immunities'; still more the talent that would fain bear the greater name, and most of all the misguided industry which is neither the one nor the other.

In this lower sphere, it is not murder and sudden death, and other such volcanic aberrations, that call for condonation ; but those

offences against that code of daily intercourse which some faulty observer of human
life has characterised as 'the minor morals.'

The type of 'genius' I am thinking of
probably began life by a misapplication, to
himself, of Emerson's essay on Self-Reliance:
a great and beautiful essay, but Oh! how
much has it to answer for in the survival of
the unfittest. Alas! that the wheat and tares
must grow together till the harvest. It is
the syrup of phosphorus by which weakly
mediocrity develops into sturdiness, a sturdy
coarseness that else might have died down
and been spared us. But, thanks to that or
some other artificial fertiliser, it grows up
with the idea that the duty which lies nearest to it is to write weary books, paint
monotonous pictures, persevere in 'd—d
bad acting'; and it fulfils that duty with an
energy known only to mediocrity. The
literary variety, probably, has the characteris-
tics of the type most fully developed. No
one takes himself with more touching seriousness. Day by day he grows in conceit,
neglects his temper, especially at home, with
a wife who is worth ten of him and all his

'works,' and generally behaves, as the phrase
goes, 'as if anything becomes him.' If you
visit him *en famille*, you will find him especially characteristic at meals, during which he
is wont to sit absorbed, with an air of 'I
cannot shake off the god'; and when they
are over he goes off, moodily chewing a
toothpick, to his den, where, maybe, the
genius finds vent in a dissertation on 'Peg-
Tops,' for *The Boy's Own*, or 'The Noses of
Great Men,' for *Chambers' Journal*.

But if such genius as this be chiefly comic,
its work cannot but awaken in one a deep
sense of the pathetic. To stand before the
poor little picture that has been so much to
its painter, and yet holds no spark of vitality
or touch of distinction ; to take up the
poor little book into which all the oil of so
many wasted days could breathe no breath
of life, formless, uninspired, unnecessary.
Think of the pathos of the illusion that has
waved 'its purple wings' around these lifeless
products, endowing with sensitive expression
the wooden lineaments that have really been
dead and unexpressive all the time, never
glowed at all save to the wistful yearning eye

of their befooled creator. Yet if nature be thus cruel to afflict, she is no less kind to console: for the victim of this species of hallucination seldom wakens from the dream. That essay on Self-Reliance is with him to the end.

Yet no less pathetic is it to reflect how his whole development has suffered for this mistake, all his life-blood gone to feed this abortive thing. The gentler charities of life have been neglected, fine qualities atrophied, the man has grown narrow and selfish, all the real things have been lost for this shadow: that he might become, what nature never meant him to be —an artist. All along, when he has made any excuse, it has been 'art.' But, more likely, he has not been asked for excuse, he has lived under the shelter of the 'genius' superstition. He has worn the air of making great sacrifices for the goddess, and in these his intimates have felt a proud sense of awful participation, as of a family whom the gods love. They have never understood that art is a particular form of self-indulgence, by no means confined to artists; that it often becomes no less a vice than opium-eating, and that the same question has to be asked of both—whether the dreams are worth the cost. This might occasionally be asked of the world's famous : not only of those whose art has been the evilly exquisite outcome of spiritual disease, but even of the great sane successful reputations.

There is, too, especially about the latter, perhaps, a touch of comic suggestiveness in the sublime preoccupation to which we owe their great legacies, that look of Atlas which is always pathetic, when it is not foolish, on the face of a mortal : the grand air of a Goethe, the colossal absorption of a Balzac. Their attitude offends one's sense of the relation of things, and we feel that, after all, we could have spared half their works for a larger share of that delicate instinct for pro- portion, which is one of the most precious attributes of what we call a gentleman. But the demi-god has always much of the *nouveau riche* about him, and a gentleman is, after all, an exquisite product. Indeed, the world has, one may think, quite enough genius to go on with. It could well do with a few more gentlemen.

A BORROWED SOVEREIGN

(TO MR. AND MRS. WELCH)

JIM lent me a sovereign. He was working hard to make his home, and was saving every penny. However, I took it, for I was really in sore straits. If you have ever known what it is absolutely to need a sovereign, when you have neither banking account nor employment, and your evening clothes are no longer accessible for the last, you will be in a position to understand the transfiguring properties of one small piece of gold. You leave your friend's rooms a different man. Like the virtuous in the Buddhistic round, you go in a beggar and come out a prince. To vary Carlyle's phrase, you can pay for dinners, you can call hansoms, you can take stalls; in fact, you are a prince—to the extent of a sovereign.

And oh! how wooingly does the world

seem to nestle round you—the same world
that was so cold and haughty ten minutes
ago.   The world is a courtesan, and has
heard you have found a sovereign.

The gaslights seem beaming love at you.
So near and bright are the streets, you want
to stay out in them all night ; though you
didn't relish the prospect last evening.   O
sweet, sweet, siren London, with your golden
voice—I have a sovereign !

This, of course, was but the first rich im-
pulse.   The sovereign should really be kept
for the lodgings.   But the snug little oyster-
shops about Booksellers' Row are so tempt-
ing, and there is nothing like oysters to give
one courage to open that giant oyster spoken
of by Ancient Pistol.

I went in.   I assured my conscience that
it should only be ' Anglo-Portuguese,' and
that I would forego the roll and butter.
But 'Anglos' are not nice, Dutch are in
every way to be preferred ; and if you are
paying eighteenpence you might as well pay
three shillings, and what's the use of drawing
the line at a roll and butter?   No! we will
repent after the roll and butter.   'Roll and

butter ' shall be my Ebenezer. The ' r's' have a notorious mnemonic quality. They will help me to remember.

So I sat down, and, fondling my sovereign in my pocket, fell into a dream. When the oysters came I wished they had been 'Anglos' after all, because my dream had grown beautiful and troublesome, and I had really forgotten the oysters altogether. However, I ate them mechanically, and ordering another half-dozen, so that the manager should not begrudge me my seat, I turned again to my dream.

A young girl sat in a dainty room, writing at a quaint old escritoire, lit by candles in shining brass sconces. She had a sweet blonde face, but more character in it than usually falls to the lot of the English girl. There was experience in the sensitive refinement of her features, a silver touch of suffering: not wasting experience or bitter suffering, but just enough to refine—she had waited. But she had been bravely happy all the time.

Pretty books filled a shelf above her escritoire, and between the candlesticks was

a photograph in a filigree silver frame. Towards this she looked every now and then,
in the pauses of her writing, with a happy,
trustful expression of quiet love. During one
pause she noticed that her little clock pointed
to 8.30. 'Jim will just be going on,' she said
to herself. Yes, that photograph was 'Jim.'

A quaint little face it was, full of sweet
wrinkles, and yet but a boy's face. The
wrinkles, you could see, were but so many
threads of gold which happy laughter had
left there. Siss called him her Punchinello,
likewise her poet, for Jim is a poet who
makes his poetry of his own bright face
and body, acts it night after night to an
audience, and the people laugh and cry as
he plays, for his face is like a bubbling
spring, full of laughing eddies on the surface,
but ever so deep with sweet freshness
beneath—and some catch sight of the deeps.
The world knows him as a comedian. Siss
knows him as a poet, and because she knows
what loving tender tears are in him as well as
laughter, she calls him her Punchinello.

This is what she was writing: 'How near
our home seems now, Jimmie boy! Every

night as you go on—and you are just going on now—I feel our home draw nearer: and, do you know, all this week our star has seemed to grow brighter and brighter. Can you see it in London? It comes out here about six o'clock—first very pale, like a dream, and then fuller and fuller and warmer and warmer. Sometimes I say that it is the sovereigns we are putting into the bank that make it so much brighter; and I am sure it *was* brighter after that last ten pounds. . . . You are laughing at me, aren't you? Never mind; you can be just as silly. Dear, dear, funny little face!'

I had reached just so far in my dream when the oysters came, and that is why I wished I had ordered 'Anglos' and no roll.

When I looked again, Siss had stopped writing, and was sitting with her head in her hands dreaming. I looked into her eyes, felt ashamed for a moment, and then stepped into her dream. I felt I was not worthy to walk there, but I took off my hat and told myself that I was reverent.

It was a pretty flat, full of dainty rooms, and I followed her from one to another, and

one there was just like that in which I had
seen her writing, with the old escritoire, and
the books, and the burning candles, and the
silver photograph shrine. She walked about
very wistfully, and her eyes were full. So
were mine, and I wanted to sob, but feared
lest she should hear. Presently Jim joined
her, and they walked together, and said to
each other, ' Think, this is our home at last '—
' Think, this is our home at last. O love, our
home—together for evermore ! '

This they said many times, and at length
they came to a room that had a door white
as ivory, and I caught a breath of freshest
flowers as they opened and passed in.

Then I closed my eyes, and when I looked
again I thought an angel stood on the
threshold, as I had seen it somewhere in
Victor Hugo—a happy angel with finger
upon his lip.

And when the dream had gone, and I was
once more alone, I said ' Jim is working, Siss
is waiting, and I—am eating borrowed
oysters.'

Then I took out the sovereign and looked
at it, for it was now symbolic. Outside, above

the street, a star was shining. I had filched
a beam of Siss's star. Was it less bright to-
night? Had she missed this sovereign?

It had been symbolic before—a sovereign's-
worth of the world, the flesh, and the devil;
now it was a sovereign's-worth of holy love
and home. Every penny I spent of it
dimmed that star, delayed that home. In
my pocket it meant a sovereign's-worth more
working and waiting. Pay it back again
into that star, and it was a sovereign nearer
home. Yes, it was a sovereign's-worth of
that flat, of that escritoire, those books, those
burning candles, that photograph, that ivory-
white door, those sweet-smelling flowers, a
sovereign's-worth of that angel, I was keeping in my pocket.

Out on it! God forgive me. I had not
thought it meant that to borrow a sovereign
from Jim, meant that to eat those borrowed
oysters. Nevertheless, they had not been
all an immoral indulgence. Even oysters
may be the instruments of virtue in the
hands of Providence.

The shopman knew me, so I 'confounded
it' and told him I had come out without my

purse. It was all right. Pay next time. Jim's theatre was close by, it was but a stone's-throw to the stage-door. Easy to leave him a note. What will he think, I wonder, as he reads it, and the sovereign rolls out: 'Dear old man, forgive me—I forgot it was a sovereign's-worth of home.'

Yet, after all, it was the oysters that did this thing.

ANARCHY IN A LIBRARY

(A FABLE FOR SOCIALISTS)

HAVING occasion recently to re-arrange my books, they lay in bewildering jumbled heaps upon my study floor; and, having in vain puzzled over this plan and that which should give the little collection a continuity such as it had never attained before, I at length gave it up in despair, and sat, with my head in my hands, hopeless. Presently I seemed to hear small voices talking in whispers, a curious papery tone, like the fluttering of leaves, and listening I heard distinctly these words :—
'The great era of universal equality and redistribution has dawned at last. No one book shall any longer claim more shelf than another, no book shall be taller or thicker than another. The age of folios and quartos is past, and the Age of the Universal Octavo has dawned.'

111

Looking up, I saw that the voice was that of a shabby, but perky, octavo, which I had forgotten I ever possessed, since the day when some mistaken charity had prompted me to rescue it from the threepenny box and give it a good home in a respectable family of books. Certainly, it had so far filled the humble position of a shelf-liner, and its accidental elevation into daylight on the top of a prostrate folio had evidently turned its head. It was now doing its best to disseminate socialistic principles among the set of scurvy octavos and duodecimos in its neighbourhood.

'Why should we choke with dust in the dark there,' it continued, 'that these splendid creatures should glitter all day in the sunshine, and get all the firelight of an evening? We were born to be read as much as they, born to enjoy our share of the good things of this world as much as my Lord Folio, as much as any Honourable Quarto, or fashionable Large Paper. My Brothers, the hour has come : will you strike now or never, exact your rights as free-born books, or will you go back to be shelf-liners as before?'

[Loud cries of 'No! no! we won't,' here encouraged the speaker.]

'Strike now, and the book unborn shall bless you. Miss this golden opportunity, and the cause we serve will be delayed another hundred editions.'

At this point a great folio that had for some time been leaning threateningly, like a slab at Stonehenge, above the speaker, suddenly fell and silenced him ; but he had not spoken in vain, and from various sets of books about the room I heard the voices of excited agitators taking up his words. Then an idea struck me. I was, as I told you, heartily sick of my task of arrangement. Here seemed an opportunity.

'Look here,' I said, 'you shall have it all to yourselves. I resign, I abdicate. You shall arrange yourselves as you please, but be quick about it, and let there be as little bloodshed as possible.'

With that there arose such a hubbub as was never before heard in a quiet book-room, not even during that famous battle of the St. James's Library in 1697 ; and conspicuous among the noises was a strange crowing

H

sound as of young cocks, which I was at a
loss to understand, till I bethought me how
Mentzelius, long ago, sitting in the quiet of
his library, had heard the bookworm 'crow
like a cock unto his mate.' On looking I saw
that the insurgents had indeed pressed into
their service a certain politic body of bookworms as joyous heralds, whom I had never
suspected of inhabiting my books at all—
though, indeed, such hidden creatures do crawl
out of their corners in times of upheaval.

It was long before I could disentangle individual voices from the wild chaos of strident
theories that surrounded me. But at last
there was silence, as one bilious-looking vellum
book, old enough to have known better, had
evidently caught the ear of the assembled
multitudes ; and then I understood that
the movement had already found its Robes-
pierre. It was clear from his words that the
universal gospel of equality, so beautifully
expatiated upon before the revolution, had
had reference only to those who were already
on an equality of that low estate which fears
no fall. The only equality now offered to
books above the rank of octavo was that of

death, which, philosophers have long assured
us, makes all men equal, by a short and
simple method. There was but one other
way—that the quartos should consent to be
cut in two, and the folios quartered ; but that,
alas ! meant death no less, for that which
alone is of worth in both books and men, the
soul, would be no more. So, as it seemed
they must die either way, all the condemned
chose death before dishonour. Several distinguished folios who, in a quixotism of
heart, had flirted with the socialistic leaders
when their schemes were but propaganda,
and equality had not yet been so rigor-
ously defined, now bitterly repented their
folly, and did their best in heading a rally
against their foes. That, however, was
soon quelled, and but hastened their
doom.

'To the guillotine with them !' cried the
bilious little octavo, and then I saw that my
tobacco-cutter had been extemporised into
the deadly engine.

But, hereupon, a voice of humour found
hearing, that of a stout 32mo, evidently a
philosopher.

'Why shed blood?' he said, 'I have a better plan. Stature is no mark of superiority, but usually the reverse. The mind's the standard of the man. In the world of men the tallest and handsomest are made into servants, and called flunkies, and these wait upon the small men, who have all the money, which among men corresponds to brains among books. Why shouldn't we take a hint from this custom, and turn these tall gaudy gentlemen into our servants, for which all their gilt and fine clothes have already provided them with livery? Ho! Sirrah Folio, come and turn my page!'

But this Lord Folio haughtily refused to do, and, consequently, being too stout to turn his own pages, the little 32mo could say no more. His proposal, though it tickled a few, found no great favour. It was generally agreed that humour had no place in the discussion of a serious question. Another speaker advocated the retention of the condemned as ornaments of the state, but he was very speedily overruled. Was not that the shallow excuse by which they had hung on for ever so long? No, that was quite worn out.

The main question was further obstructed by many outbursts of individualism. Certain self-contained books wished to be left to themselves, and have no part in the social scheme, unless in the event of a return to monarchy, when, they intimated, they might be eligible for election. This, one could see, was the secret hope of all the speakers ; and you would have laughed could you have heard what inflated opinions some of them had of their own importance—especially two or three of the minor poets. Then, again, many sentimental demands, quite unforeseen, added to the general anarchy. Collected editions, which had long groaned in the bondage of an arbitrary relationship, saw an opportunity in the general overturn to break away from their sets and join their natural fellows. Sex was naturally the most unruly element of all. Volumes that had waited edition after edition for each other, yearning across the shelves, felt their time had come at last, and leapt into each other's arms. It was with no avail that a distress minute was passed by The

Hundred Thousand Committee (a somewhat unworkable body) that henceforth sex was to be a function exercised absolutely for the good of the state : tattered poets were to be seen wildly proclaiming a different doctrine.

Such eccentric attachments as a volume of *The Essays of Elia* for Margaret, Duchess of Newcastle, were especially troublesome ; while the explosion caused by the accidental contact of that same unruly Elia with a modern reprint of *The Anatomy of Melancholy*, which (he said) he never could tolerate, proved the last straw to the Committee of the Hundred Thousand, who immediately resigned their offices in anger and despair. Thereupon, tenfold chaos once more returning, I thought it time to interfere. The Doctrine of Equality was evidently a failure—among books, at any rate. So I savagely fell to, and threw the books back again into their immemorial places, and the cause of freedom in 'The City of Books' sleeps for another hundred editions.

Only I placed Elia next to the Duchess, because he was a human fellow and had no theories.

THE PHILOSOPHY OF
'LIMITED EDITIONS'

WHY do the heathen so furiously rage against limited issues, large - papers, first editions, and the rest? For there is certainly more to be said for than against them. Broadly speaking, all such 'fads' are worthy of being encouraged, because they maintain, in some measure, the expiring dignity of letters, the mystery of books. Day by day the wonderfulness of life is becoming lost to us. The sanctities of religion are defiled, the 'fairy tales' of science have become commonplaces. Christian mysteries are debased in the streets to the sound of drum and trumpet, and the sensitive ear of the telephone is but a servile drudge 'twixt speculative bacon merchants. And Books!—those miraculous memories of high thoughts and golden moods; those magical shells tremulous with

the secrets of the ocean of life; those love-
letters that pass from hand to hand of a
thousand lovers that never meet; those
honeycombs of dreams; those orchards of
knowledge ; those still-beating hearts of the
noble dead ; those mysterious signals that
beckon along the darksome pathways of the
past; voices through which the myriad
lispings of the earth find perfect speech;
oracles through which its mysteries call like
voices in moonlit woods ; prisms of beauty;
urns stored with all the sweets of all the
summers of time ; immortal nightingales that
sing for ever to the rose of life : Books, Bibles
—ah me! what have ye become to-day!

What, indeed, has become of that mystery
of the Printed Word, of which Carlyle so
movingly wrote? It has gone, it is to be
feared, with those Memnonian mornings we
sleep through with so determined snore, those
ancient mysteries of night we forget beneath
the mimic firmament of the music-hall.

Only in the lamplit closet of the bookman,
the fanatic of first and fine editions, is it
remembered and revered. To him alone of
an Americanised, 'pirated-edition' reading

world, the book remains the sacred thing it is. Therefore, he would not have it degraded by, so to say, an indiscriminate breeding, such as has also made the children of men cheap and vulgar to each other. We pity the desert rose that is born to unappreciated beauty, the unset gem that glitters on no woman's hand; but what of the book that eats its heart out in the threepenny box, the remainders that are sold ignominiously in job lots by ignorant auctioneers? Have we no feeling for them?

Over-production, in both men and shirts, is the evil of the day. The world has neither enough food, nor enough love, for the young that are born into it. We have more mouths than we can fill, and more books than we can buy. Well, the publisher and collector of limited editions aim, in their small corner, to set a limit to this careless procreation. They are literary Malthusians. The ideal world would be that in which there should be at least one lover for each woman. In the higher life of books the ideal is similar. No book should be brought into the world, which is not sure of love and lodging on some comfortable shelf. If writers and publishers only gave a thought to what they are doing, when they generate such large families of books, careless as the salmon with its million young, we should have no such sad almshouses of learning as Booksellers' Row, no such melancholy distress-sales of noble authors as remainder auctions. A good book is beyond price; and it is far easier to under than over sell it. The words of the modern minor poet are as rubies, and what if his sets bring a hundred guineas?—it is more as it should be, than that any sacrilegious hand should fumble them for threepence. It recalls that golden age of which Mr. Dobson has sung, when—

> ' . . . a book was still a Book,
> Where a wistful man might look,
> Finding something through the whole
> Beating—like a human soul';

days when for one small gilded manuscript men would willingly exchange broad manors, with pasture lands, chases, and blowing woodlands; days when kings would send anxious embassies across the sea, burdened with rich gifts to abbot and prior, if haply gold might purchase a single poet's book.

But, says the scoffer, these limited editions and so forth foster the vile passions of competition. Well, and if they do? Is it not meet that men should strive together for such possessions? We compete for the allotments of shares in American-meat companies, we outbid each other for tickets 'to view the Royal procession,' we buffet at the gate of the football field, and enter into many another of the ignoble rivalries of peace; and are not books worth a scrimmage?—books that are all those wonderful things so poetically set forth in a preceding paragraph! Lightly earned, lightly spurned, is the sense, if not the exact phrasing, of an old proverb. There is no telling how we should value many of our possessions if they were more arduously come by: our relatives, our husbands and wives, our presentation poetry from the unpoetical, our invitation-cards to one-man shows in Bond Street, the auto-photographs of great actors, the flatteries of the unimportant, the attentions of the embarrassing: how might we not value all such treasures, if they were, so to say, restricted to a limited issue, and guaranteed 'not to be reprinted'—'plates destroyed and type distributed.'

Indeed, all nature is on the side of limited editions. Make a thing cheap, she cries from every spring hedgerow, and no one values it. When do we find the hawthorn, with its breath sweet as a milch-cow's; or the wild rose, with its exquisite attar and its petals of hollowed pearl—when do we find these decking the tables of the great? or the purple bilberry, or the boot-bright blackberry in the entremets thereof? Think what that 'common dog-rose' would bring in a limited edition! And new milk from the cow, or water from the well! Where would champagne be if those intoxicants were restricted by expensive licence, and sold in gilded bottles? What would you not pay for a ticket to see the moon rise, if nature had not improvidently made it a free entertainment; and who could afford to buy a seat at Covent Garden if Sir Augustus Harris should suddenly become sole impresario of the nightingale?

Yes, 'from scarped cliff and quarried stone,' Nature cries, 'Limit the Edition! Distribute the type!'—though in her capacity as the great publisher, she has been all too prodigal of her issues, and ruinously guilty of innumerable remainders. In fact, it is by her warning rather than by her example that we must be guided in this matter. Let us not vulgarise our books, as she has done her stars and flowers. Let us, if need be, make our editions smaller and smaller, our prices increasingly 'prohibitive,' rather than that we should forget the wonder and beauty of printed dream and thought, and treat our books as somewhat less valuable than wayside weeds.

A PLEA FOR THE OLD PLAYGOER

HE'S a nuisance, of course. But to see only that side of him is to think, as the shepherd boy piped, 'as though' you will 'never grow old.' Does he never appeal to you with any more human significance, a significance tearful and uncomfortably symbolic? Or are you so entirely that tailor's fraction of manhood, the *fin de siècle* type, that your ninth part does not include a heart and the lachrymal gland?

You suspect him at once as you squeeze past his legs to your stall, for he cannot quite conceal the hissing twinge of gout; and you are hardly seated ere you are quite sure that a long night of living for others is before you.

'You hardly would think it, perhaps,' he begins, 'but I saw Charles Young play the part—yes, in 1824.'

If you are young and innocent, you think —'What an interesting old gentleman!' and you have vague ideas of pumping him for reminiscences to turn into copy. Poor boy, you soon find that there is no need of pumping on your part. He is entirely self-acting, and the wells of his autobiography are as deep as the foundations of the world.

If you are more experienced, you make a quick frantic effort to escape ; you try to nip the bud of his talk with a frosty 'indeed!' and edge away, calling upon your programme to cover you. You never so much as turn the sixteenth part of an eye in his direction, for even as the oyster-man, should the poor mollusc heave the faintest sigh, is inside with his knife in the twinkling of a star ; even as a beetle has but to think of moving its tiniest leg for the bird to swoop upon him,—even so will the least muscular interest in your neighbour give you bound hand and foot into his power.

But really and truly escape is hopeless. You are beyond the reach of any salvage agency whatsoever. Better make up your

mind to be absolutely rude or absolutely
kind : and the man who can find in his heart
to be the former must have meeting eye-
brows, and will sooner or later be found
canonised in wax at Madame Tussaud's. To
be the latter, however, is by no means easy.
It is one of the most poignant forms of self-
sacrifice attained by the race. In that, at
least, you have some wintry consolation ; and
the imaginative vignette of yourself wearing
the martyr's crown is a pretty piece of sacred
art.

If you wished to make a bag of old play-
goers, or meditated a sort of Bartholomew's
Eve, a revival of *Hamlet* would, of course,
be the occasion you would select for your
purpose: for the old playgoer, so to speak,
collects Hamlets. At a first night of *Hamlet*
every sixth stall-holder is a Dr. Doran up to
date, his mind a portfolio of old prints.

That is why a perambulation of the stalls
is as perilous as to pick one's way through
hot ploughshares. You can hardly hope
always to pass through unscathed. You
are as sure some night to find yourself
seated beside him, as you will some

day be called to serve on the jury. And then—

'O limèd soul, that, struggling to be free,
Art more engaged!'

However, 'sudden the worst turns best to the brave,' and 'there is much music' in this old fellow if only you have the humanity to listen.

To begin with, he has probably a distinguished face, with a bunch of vigorous curly hair, white as hawthorn. He has a manner, too. Suppose you try and enter into his soul for a moment. It does us good to get outside ourselves for a while, and this old man's soul is a palace of memory. Those lines that, maybe, have been familiar to you for sixteen years, have been familiar to him for sixty. That is why he knows them off so well, why he repeats them under his breath—Look at his face!—like a Methodist praying, anticipating the actor in all the fine speeches. Do look at his face! How it shines, as the golden passages come treading along. How his head moves in an ecstasy of remembrance, in which there is a whole world of tears. How he half turns to you

I

with a wistful appeal to feel what he is feeling: an appeal that might kindle a clod. It is the old wine laughing to itself within the old bottle.

And, one thing you will notice, it is the poetry that moves him : the great metaphor, the sonorous cadence, the honeysuckle fancy. He belongs to an age that had an instinct for beauty, and loved style—an age that, in the words of a modern wit, had not grown all nose with intellect, an age that went to the theatre to dream, not to dissect.

For you there may be here and there a flower of remembrance stuck within the leaves of the play, but for him it is stained through with the sweets of sixty springs. His youth lies buried within it like a thousand violets.

Practically he is Death at the play. To you there is but one ghost in *Hamlet*, to him there are fifty, and they all dance like shadows behind 'the new Hamlet,' and even sit about the stalls.

If your love be with you, forbear to press her hand in the love-scenes, or, at least, don't let the old man see you : because he used to punctuate those very passages he is muttering, in just the same way—sixty years ago, when she whose angel face he will kiss no more, unless it be in the heavenly fields, sat like a flower at his side. Poor old fellow, can you be selfish to him? Can you say, ' These tedious old fools!' Fool thyself, this night shall thy youth be required of thee.

You might think of this next time you drop across the old playgoer. It was natural in Hamlet to swear at Polonius—who, you will remember, was an old playgoer himself —but, being a gentleman, it was natural in him, too, to recall the first player with, 'Follow that lord; but look you mock him not!'

THE MEASURE OF A MAN

I SOMETIMES grow melancholy with the thought that, though I wear trousers and shave once a day, I am not, properly speaking, a Man. Surely it is from no failure of goodwill, no lack of prayerful striving towards that noble estate: for if there is one spectacle in this moving phantasmagoria of life that I love to carry within my eye, it is the figure of a true man. The mere idea of a true man stirs one's heart like a trumpet. Therefore, this doubt I am confiding is all the more dreary. Naturally, I feel it most keenly in the company of my fellows, each one of whom seems to carry the victorious badge of manhood, as though to cry shame upon me. They make me shrink into myself, make me feel that I am but an impostor in their midst. Indeed, in that sensitiveness of mine you have the starting-point of my unmanliness. Look at that noble fellow there. He is six-foot odd in his stockings, straight, stalwart, and confident. His face is broad and strong, his close-cropped head is firm and proud on his shoulders—firm and proud as a young bull's. It is a head made, indeed, rather to butt than to think with ; it is visited with no effeminacy of thought or dream. It has another striking quality : it is hardly distinguishable from any other head in the room—for I am in an assemblage of true men all, a glorious herd of young John Bulls. All have the same strong jaws, the same powerful low foreheads. Noble fellows ! Any one of them could send me to eternity with the wind of his fist.

And, most of all, is their manhood brought home to me, with a sickening sense of inferiority, in their voices. What a leonine authority in the roar of their opinions ! Their words strike the air firm as the tread of lions. They are not teased with fine distinctions, possibilities of misconception, or the perils of afterthought. Their talk is of the absolute, their opinions wear the primary colours, and dream not of 'art

shades.' Never have they been wrong in
their lives, never shall they be wrong in the
time to come. Never have they been known
to conjecture that another may, after all, be
wiser than they, handsomer, stronger, or
more fortunate. They would kill a man
rather than admit a mistake. Noble fellows!
And I? Do you wonder that I blush in my
corner as I gaze upon them, strive to smooth
my hair into the appearance of a manly
flatness, strive to set my face hard and feign
it knowing, strive to elevate my voice to the
dogmatic note, strive to cast out from my
mind all those evil spirits of proportion?

Can it be possible that any one of my
readers has ever been in a like case? Is
there hope for us, my brother? You have, I
perceive, a fine, expressive, sensitive counten-
ance. That is, indeed, against you in this
race for manhood. It is true that Apollo
passed for a man—but that was long ago,
and not in Britain. You have a pleasant,
sympathetic voice. An excellent thing in
woman. But you, my friend,—break it, I
beseech you. Coarsen it with raw spirits
and rawer opinions; and set that face of

thine with hog's bristles, plant a shoe-brush
on thy upper lip, and send thy head to the
turner of billiard balls. Else come not nigh
me, for, 'fore Heaven, I love a man !

Sometimes, however, I am inclined to a
more comfortable consideration of this great
question—for it is one of my weaknesses to
be positive on few matters. But to-day I
taunted my soul with its unmanliness till it
rose in rebellion against me. ' Poor-spirited
creature,' I said, ' where is thy valour ?
When a fool has struck thee I have seen thee
pass on without a word, not so much as a
momentary knitting of thy fist. When
ignorance has waxed proud, and put thee
to the mock, thou hast sat meek, and uttered
never a word. It must needs be thou
art pigeon-livered and lack gall ! There
is not in thee the swagger, the rustle, the
braggadocio of a true swashbuckler manhood.
Out on thee !'

And my soul took the blows in patience.

' Hast thou any courage hid in any crevice
of thee ?' I continued my taunt. And
suddenly my soul answered with a firm quiet
voice : 'Try me !'

Then said I, 'Coward as thou art, fearful
of thy precious skin, darest thou strike a
blow for the weak against his oppressor,
darest thou meet the strong tyrant in the
way?'

And thereon I was startled, for my soul
suddenly sprang up within me, and, lo! it
neighed like a war-horse for the battle.

'Ah!' I continued, 'but couldst thou fight
against the enemy of thy land? Surely thy
valour would melt at the clash of swords and
the voice of the drum?'

And the answer of my soul was like the
march of armed men.

Then said I softly, for ı was touched by
this unwonted valour of my soul, 'Soul!
wouldst thou die for thy friend?'

And the voice of my soul came sweet as
the sound of bells at evening. It seemed,
indeed, as though it could dream of naught
sweeter than to die for one's friend.

This colloquy of inner and outer set me
further reflecting. Can it be that this manhood is, after all, rather a quality of the
spirit than of the body; that it is to be
sought rather in the stout heart than in the

strong arm ; that big words and ready blows
may, like a display of bunting, betoken no
true loyalty, and be but the gaudy sign to a
sorry inn ? Dr. Watts, it may be remembered, declared the mind to be the standard
of the man. As he was the author of a book
on 'The Human Mind,' envious persons
may meanly conceive that his statement was
but a subtly-disguised advertisement of his
literary wares.

> ' Were I so tall to reach the Pole,
>   Or grasp the ocean in my span,
> I must be measured by my soul :
>   The mind 's the standard of the man.'

The fact of Dr. Watts being also a man of
low stature does not affect the truth or un-
truth of this fine verse, which may serve to
comfort many. One may assume that it was
Jack, and not the giant, whom we would
need to describe as the true man of the two ;
and one seems to have heard of some 'fine,'
'manly' fellows, darlings of the football
field and the American bar, whose actions
somehow have not altogether justified those
epithets, or, at any rate, certain readings of
them. Theirs is a manhood. one fancies.

that is given to shine more at race-meetings and in hotel parlours than at home—revealed to the bar-maid, and strangely hidden from the wife, who, indeed, has less opportunities for perceiving it.

This kind of manhood is, perhaps, rather a fashion than a personal quality : a way of carrying the stick, of wearing, or not wearing, the hair; it resides in the twirl of the moustache, or the cut of the trouser ; you must seek it in the quality of the boot and the shape of the hat rather than in the actions of the wearer.

Take that matter of the hair. When next the street-boy sorrowfully exclaims on your passing that 'it's no wonder the barbers all 'list for soldiers,' or some puny idiot at your club—a lilliputian model of popular 'manhood'—sniggers to his friend behind his coffee as you come in : call to mind pictures of certain brave 'tailed men' of old, at the winking of whose eyelid your tiny club 'man' would have expired on the instant. Threaten him with a Viking. Show him in a vision a band of blue-eyed pirates, with their wild hair flying in the breeze, as they sternly

hasten across the Northern Sea. Summon
Godiva's lord, 'his beard a yard before him,
and his hair a yard behind.' Call up the
brave picture of Rupert's love-locked Cava-
liers, as their glittering column hurls like a
bolt of heaven to the charge, or Nelson's
pig-tailed sailors in Trafalgar's Bay. But,
before you have gone half-way through
your panorama, that club-mannikin will
have hastily departed, leaving his coffee
half-drunk, and you shall find him airing
his manhood in the security of the billiard-
room.

Yes, for us who are denied the admiration
of the billiard-marker; denied the devotion
of the bar-maid (with charming paradox so-
called); for us who make poor braggarts,
and often prefer to surrender rather than to
elbow for our rights; for us who deliver our
opinions with mean-spirited diffidence, and
are men of quiet voices and ways: for us
there is hope. It may be that to love one's
neighbour is also a part of manhood, to
suffer quietly for another as true a piece of
bravery as to fell him for a careless word;
it may be that purity, constancy, and rever-

ence are as sure criteria of manhood as their opposites. It may be, I say; but be certain that a strong beard, a harsh voice, and a bull-dog physiognomy are surer still.

THE BLESSEDNESS OF WOMAN

HAVE you ever remarked as a curious thing that, whereas every day we hear women sighing because they have not been born men, you never hear a sigh blowing in the other direction ? I only know one man who had the courage to say that he would not mind exchanging into the female infantry, and it may have been affectation on his part. At any rate, he blushed deeply at the avowal, and his friends look askance at him ever since. Of course, the obvious answer of the self-satisfied male is that he is the lord of creation, that his is the better part which shall not be taken from him. Yet this does not prevent his telling his wife sometimes, when oppressed with the cares of this world and the deceitfulness of riches, that ' it is nice to be her. Nothing to worry her all day long. No responsibility.' For in his primitive vision of female existence, his wife languidly presides for ever at an eternal five-o'clock tea. And it is not in the province of this article to turn to him the seamy side of that charming picture. Rather is it our mission to convince him of the substantial truth of his intuition. He is quite right. It *is* 'nice to be her.' And if men had a little more common-sense in their consequential skulls, instead of striving to resist the woman's invasion of their immemorial responsibilities and worries, they would joyfully abdicate them—and skip home to Nirvâna and afternoon tea.

Foolish women! To want of your own free will to put yourselves in painful harness; to take the bit of servitude between your rose-leaf lips; to fight day-long in the reeking arena of bacon merchants; to settle accounts instead of merely incurring them; to be confined in Stygian city-blocks instead of silken bedchambers; to rise with the sparrow and leave by the early morning train. What fatuity! Some day, when woman has had her way and man has ceased

to have his will, she will see of the travail
of her soul and be bitterly dissatisfied ; for,
unless man is a greater fool than he looks,
she shall demand back her petticoats in
vain.

For what is the lot of woman ? The first
superficial fact about a woman is, of course,
her beauty. Secondly, as the leaves about a
rose, comes her dress. To be beautiful and
to wear pretty things—these are two of the
obvious privileges of woman. To be a
living rose, with bosom of gold and petals of
lace, a rose each passer-by longs to pluck
from its husband-stem, but dare not for fear
of the husband-thorns. To be privileged to
play Narcissus all day long with your mirror,
to love yourself so much that you kiss the
cold reflection, yet fear not to drown. To
reveal yourself to yourself in a thousand
lovely poses, and bird-like poises of the head.
To kneel to yourself in adoration, to laugh
and nod and beckon to yourself with your
own smiles and dimples, to yearn in hopeless
passion for your own loveliness. To finger
silken garments, linings to the casket of your
beauty, never seen of men, to draw on stiff

embroidered gowns, to deck your hands with
glittering jewels, and your wrists with bands
of gold—and then to sail forth from your
boudoir like the moon from a cloud, regally
confident of public worship ; to be at once
poet and poem, painter and painted : does
not this belong to the lot of woman ?

But it was of nobler privileges than these
that the candidate for womanhood of whom
I have spoken was thinking. It is fit that
we skim the surface before we dive into the
deeps—especially so attractive a surface as
woman's. He was, doubtless, thinking less
of woman as a home comfort or a beauty,
and much more of her as she once used to be
among our far-off sires, Sibyl and Priestess.
Is it but an insular fancy to suppose that
Englishmen, beyond any other race, still
retain the most living faith in the sanctity of
womanhood ? and, if so, can it be doubted
that it is an inheritance from those wild
child-hearted Vikings, who were first among
the peoples of Europe to conceive woman as
the chosen vessel of the divine ? And how
wittily true, by the way, how slily significant,
was both the Norse and the Greek concep-

tion of the ruling destinies of man, the Norns
and the Fates, as women!

To speak with authority, one should,
doubtless, first sprout petticoats ; and, meanwhile, one must rest content with asking
the intelligent women of our acquaintance
—whether man inspires them with anything
like the feelings of reverential adoration,
the sense of a being holy and supernal,
with which woman undoubtedly inspires
man. He is, of course, their god, but a god
of the Greek pattern, with no little of the
familiarising alloy of earth in his composition.
He is strong, and swift, and splendid—but
seems he holy ? Is he angel as well as god ?
Does the dream of him rise silvery in the
imagination of woman ? Is he a star to lift
her up to heaven with pure importunate beam?
I seem to hear the nightingale-laughter of
women for answer. Man neither is, nor
would they have him, any of these things.

But though some men, by a fortunate admix-
ture of woman silver in their masculine clay,
may be even these, there is one sacred thing
no man can ever be, a privilege by which
nature would seem to have put beyond doubt

K

the divinity of woman : a mother. It is true
that it is within his reach to be a father ; but
what is 'paternity' compared with motherhood ? The very word wears a droll face, as
though accustomed to banter. Let us venture
on the bull : that, though it be possible for
most men to be fathers, no man can ever be
a mother. Maybe a recondite intention of
the dogma of the Immaculate Conception
was the accentuation of the fact that man's
share in the sacred mystery of birth is so
small and woman's so great, that the birth of
a child is truly a mysterious traffic between
divine powers of nature and her miraculous
womb—mystic visitations of radiant forces
hidden eternally from the knowledge of man.

We stand in wonder before the magical
germinating properties of a clod of earth. A
grass-seed and a thimbleful of soil set all the
sciences at nought. But if such is the wonder
of the mere spectator, how strange to be the
very vessel of the mystery, to know it moving
through its mystic stations within our very
bodies, to feel the tender shoots of the young
life striking out blade after blade, already
living and wonderful, though as yet unsus-

pected of other eyes; to know the underground inarticulate spring, sweeter far than
spring of bird and blossom, while as yet all
seems barren winter in the upper air; to hear
already the pathetic pleadings of the young
life, and to send back soothing answer along
the hidden channels of tender tremulous affini-
ties; to lie still in the night and see through
the darkness the little white soul shining
softly in its birth-sleep, slowly filling with life
as a moon with silver—it was a woman and
not a man that God chose for this blessedness.

VIRAGOES OF THE BRAIN

THE strength of the old-fashioned virago was in her muscles. That of the new-fangled modern development is in her 'reason'—a very different thing indeed from 'woman's reasons.' As the former knocked you down with her fist, the latter fells you with her brain. In her has definitely commenced that evolutionary process which, according to the enchanting dream of a recent scientist, is to make the 'homo' a creature whose legs are of no account, poor shrivelled vestiges of once noble calves and thighs; and whose entire significance will be a noseless, hairless head, in shape and size like an idiot's, which the scientist, gloating over the ugly duckling of his distorted imagination, describes as a 'beautiful, glittering, hairless dome!' A sad period one fears for Gaiety burlesque. In that day

148

a beautifully shaped leg and a fine head of hair will be rather a disgrace than a distinction. They will be survivals of a barbarous age. Indeed that they are already so regarded, there can be no doubt, by the more 'advanced' representatives of the female sex.

There is one radical difference between the old and the new virago : the old gloried in the fact that she was a woman, because thus her sex triumphed over that male whom she despised, like her modern sister, in proportion as she resembled him. The new virago, however, hates above all things to be reminded of her womanhood, which she is constantly engaged in repressing with Chinese ferocity. Not, as we have hinted, that she thinks any better of man. Though she dresses as like him as possible, she is very angry if you suggest that she at all envies him his birthright. And the humour of the situation, the hopeless dilemma in which she thus places herself— if it be right to apply the feminine gender! — never occurs to one whose sense of humour has long been atrophied, perhaps at Girton, or by a course of sterilising Extension lectures.

Obviously, there is but one course open for the advanced 'woman' in this dilemma —to evolve a third sex ; and this she is doing her best to achieve, with, I am bound to admit, remarkably speedy success. The result up to date is the Virago of the Brain, or the Female Frankenstein. The patentees of this fearsome *tertium quid* hope to present it to their patrons, within a very few years, in a form entirely devoid of certain physiological defects, with which the cussedness of human structure still uselessly burdens the Virago. As it is, of course, it is by no means uncommon for the virago to be born without that sentimental organ, the heart ; and it can, therefore, only be a matter of time before she is rid of what the present writer has been criticised for calling ' her miraculous womb.' Doubtless, the patentees will then turn their attention to Sir Thomas Browne's suggested method for the propagation of the race after the reasonable, civilised, and advanced manner of trees.

But I am warned that I commit impropriety even in naming such matters. They are 'sacred,'—which means that we ought to be ashamed to mention them, however reverent our intention. Motherhood, it would appear, is not, as one had regarded it, a sanctifying privilege, but a shameful disability, of which not the Immaculate Conception, but the ignoble service for the 'purification' of women, is the significant symbol. It behoves not only the unmarried, but the married mothers, so to speak, to wear farthingales upon the subject, and pretend, with as grave a face as possible, that babies are really found under cabbages, or sent parcel post, on application, by her Majesty the Queen.

How long are we to retain the pernicious fallacy that sacredness is a quality inhering not in the sacred object itself, but in the superstitious 'decencies' that swaddle it, or that we best reverence such sacred object by a prurient prudish conspiracy of silence concerning it?

Then there is, it would also appear, a particular indignity, from the new virago's point of view, in the assumption that a

woman's beauty is one of her great missions,
or the supposition that she takes any such
pride in it herself as man has from time
immemorial supposed. No sensible woman,
we have been indignantly assured, ever
plays at Narcissus with her mirror. That
all women find such pleasure in their reflections no one would think of saying. How
could they, poor things ? One is quite
ready to admit that probably our virago
looks in her glass as seldom as possible.
But all sensible women that are beautiful as
well should take joy in their own charms, if
they have any feelings of gratitude towards
the supernal powers which might have made
them—well, more advanced than beautiful,
and given them a head full of cheap philo-
sophy instead of a transfiguring head of
hair.

No one wants a woman to be silly and
vain about her beauty. But vanity and
conceit are qualities that exist in people
quite independently of their gifts and
graces. The ugly and stupid are perhaps
more often conceited than the beautiful or
the clever,—vain, it would appear, of their

very ugliness and stupidity. Besides, is it any worse for a woman to be vain of her looks than of her brains?—and the advanced woman is without doubt most inordinately vain of those. Of the two, so far as they are at present developed, is there any doubt that the woman with beauty is better off than the woman with brains? In some few hundred years, maybe, the brain of woman will be a joy to herself and the world : when she has got more used to its possession, and familiar with the fruitful control of it. At present, however, it is merely a discomfort, not to say a danger, to herself and every one else—a tiresome engine for the pedantic assimilation of German and the higher mathematics. And it may well happen—horrid prophecy—that when that brain of woman has come to its perfection, the flower of its meditation will be to realise the significance, the sacredness, of the Simple Woman. It is in its apprehension of the mystery of simplicity that the brain of man, at present, is superior to that of woman.

Young brain delights in the complex, old

in the simple. Woman's love of the complex has been illustrated abundantly during
the last few years, in her enthusiasm for
certain great imperfect writers, who have
been able to stir up the mud in the fountain
of life (doubtless, to medicinal ends) but
unable to bring it clear again. An eternal
enigma herself, woman is eternally in love
with enigmas. Like a child, she loves any
one who will show her the 'works' of existence, and she is still in that inquisitive stage
when one imagines that the inside of a doll
will afford explanation of its fascinating
exterior. It is no use telling her that
analysis can never explain the mystery of
synthesis. Like an American humourist, she
still goes on wanting 't' know.'

Even more than man, she exaggerates the
value of the articulate, the organised. She has
always been in love with 'accomplishments,'
and she loves natures that are minted into
current coin of ready gifts and graces. She
cares more for the names of things than for the
things themselves. Of things without names
she is impatient. Talkative as she is said to
be, and in so many modern languages, she

knows not yet how to talk with Silence—unless she be the inspired Simple Woman—for to talk with Silence is to apprehend the mystic meanings of simplicity. For this reason, mystics are more often found among men than women — a fact on which the Pioneer Club is at liberty to congratulate itself. What advanced woman understands that saying of Paracelsus : ' who tastes a crust of bread tastes the heavens and all the stars.' Else would she understand also that the ' humblest' ministrations of life, those nearest to nature, are the profoundest in their significance : that it means as much to bake a loaf as to write a book, and that to watch over the sleep of a child is a liberal education — nay, an initiation granted only to mothers and those meek to whom mysteries are revealed. It has always been to the simple woman that the angel has appeared— to Mary of Bethany, to Joan of Arc. Is it impious to infer that the Angel Gabriel himself dreads a blue-stocking ? What chance indeed would he have with our modern viragoes of the brain, the mighty daughters of the pen ?

THE EYE OF THE
BEHOLDER

OTHER people's poetry—I don't mean their published verse, but their absurdly romantic view of unromantic objects—is terribly hard to translate. It seldom escapes being turned into prose. It must have happened to you now and again to have had the photograph of your friend's beloved produced for your inspection and opinion. It is a terrible moment. If she does happen to be a really pretty girl—heavens! what a relief. You praise her with almost hysterical gratitude. But if, as is far more likely, her beauty proves to be of that kind which exists only in the eyes of a single beholder, what a plight is yours! How you strive to look as if she were a new Helen, and how hopelessly unconvincing is your weary expression—as unconvincing as one's expression when, having weakly pretended acquaintance with a strange author, we feign ecstatic recognition of some passage or episode quoted by his ruthless admirer. There is this hope in the case of the photograph: that its amorous possessor will probably be incapable of imagining any one insensitive to such a Golconda of charms, and you have always in your power the revenge of showing him your own sacred graven image.

Is it not curious that ·the very follies we delight in for ourselves should seem so stupid, so absolutely vulgar, when practised by others? The last illusion to forsake a man is the absolute belief in his own refinement.

A test experience in other people's poetry is to sit in the pit of a theatre and watch 'Arry and 'Arriet making love and eating oranges simultaneously. 'Arry has a low forehead, close, black, oily hair, his eyes and nose are small, and his face is freckled. His clothes are painfully his best, he wears an irrelevant flower, and his tie has escaped from the stud and got high into his neck, eclipsing his collar. 'Arriet has thick unexpressive features, relying rather on the expressiveness of her flaunting hat, she wears a straight fringe low down on her forehead, and endeavours to disguise her heavy *ennui* by an immovable simper. This pair loll one upon each other. Whether lights be high or low they hold each other's hands, hands hard and coarse with labour, with nails bitten down close to the quick. But, for all that, they, in their strange uncouth fashion, would seem to be loving each other. 'Not we alone have passions hymeneal,' sings an aristocratic poet. They smile at each other, an obvious animal smile, and you perhaps shudder. Or you study them for a realistic novel, or you call up that touch of nature our great poet talks of. But somehow you cannot forget how their lips will stick and smell of oranges when they kiss each other on the way home. What is the truth about this pair? Is it in the unlovely details on which, maybe, we have too much insisted—or behind these are we to imagine their souls radiant in celestial nuptials?

Mr. Chevalier may be said to answer the

question in his pictures of coster love-making.
But are those pictures to be taken as docu-
ments, or are they not the product of Mr.
Chevalier's idealistic temperament? Does
the coster actually worship his 'dona' with
so fine a chivalry? Is he so sentimentally
devoted to his 'old Dutch'? If you answer
the question in the negative, you are in this
predicament: all the love and 'the fine feelings' remain with the infinitesimal residuum
of the cultured and professionally 'refined.'
Does that residuum actually incarnate all the
love, devotion, honour, and other noble
qualities in man? One need hardly trouble
to answer the absurd question. Evidently
behind the oranges, and the uncouth animal
manners, we should find souls much like our
own refined essences, had we the seeing .
sympathetic eye. All depends on the eye of
the beholder.

Among the majority of literary and artistic
people of late that eye of the beholder has
been a very cynical supercilious eye. Never
was such a bitter cruel war waged against
the poor *bourgeois*. The lack of humanity in
recent art and literature is infinitely depress-

ing. Doubtless, it is the outcome of a so-called 'realism,' which dares to pretend that the truth about life is to be found on its grimy pock-marked surface. Over against the many robust developments of democracy, and doubtless inspired by them, is a marked spread of the aristocratic spirit—selfish, heartless, subtle, of mere physical 'refinement'; a spirit, too, all the more inhuman because it is for the most part not tempered by any intercourse with homely dependants, as in the feudal aristocracy. It would seem to be the product of 'the higher education,' a university priggishness, poor as proud. It is the deadliest spirit abroad ; but, of course, though it may poison life and especially art for a while, the great laughing democracy will in good time dispose of it as Hercules might crush a wasp.

This is the spirit that draws up its skirts and sneers to itself at poor 'old bodies' in omnibuses, because, forsooth, they are stout, and out of the fulness of the heart the mouth speaketh. One thinks of Falstaff's plaintive 'If to be fat is to be hated!' At displays of natural feelings of any sort this comfortless evil spirit ever curls the lip. Inhabiting modern young ladies, it is especially superior to the maternal instinct, and cringes from a baby in a railway carriage as from an adder. At the dropping of an 'h' it shrinks as though the weighty letter had fallen upon its great toe, and it will forgive anything rather than a provincial accent. It lives entirely in the surfaces of things, and, as the surface of life is frequently rough and prickly, it is frequently uncomfortable. At such times it peevishly darts out its little sting, like a young snake angry with a farmer's boot. It is amusing to watch it venting its spleen in papers the *bourgeois* never read, in pictures they don't trouble to understand. John Bull's indifference to the ' new' criticism is one of the most pleasing features of the time. Probably he has not yet heard a syllable of it, and, if he should hear, he would probably waive it aside with, ' I have something more to think of than these megrims.' And so he has. While these superior folk are wrangling about Dégas and Mallarmé, about 'style' and 'distinction,' he is doing the

work of the world. There is nothing in life
so much exaggerated as the importance of art.
If it were all wiped off the surface of the
earth to-morrow, the world would scarcely
miss it. For what is art but a faint reflection
of the beauty already sown broadcast over
the face of the world? And that would remain. We should lose Leonardo and Titian,
Velasquez and Rembrandt, and a great
host of modern precious persons, but the
stars and the great trees, the noble sculptured
hills, the golden-dotted meadows, the airy
sailing clouds, and all the regal pageantry of
the seasons, would still be ours ; and an
almond-tree in flower would replace the
National Gallery.

Yes, surely the true way of contemplating
these undistinguished masses of humanity,
this ' h ' dropping, garlic-eating, child-beget-
ting *bourgeois*, is Shakespeare's, Dickens',
Whitman's way—through the eye of a gentle
sympathetic beholder—one who understands
Nature's trick of hiding her most precious
things beneath rough husks and in rank and
bearded envelopes — and not through the
eye-glass of the new critic.

For these undistinguished people are, after all, alive as their critics are not. They are, indeed, the only people who may properly be said to be alive, dreaming and building while the superior person stands by cogitating sarcasms on their swink'd and dusty appearances. More of the true spirit of romantic existence goes to the opening of a little grocer's shop in a back street in Whitechapel than to all the fine marriages at St. George's, Hanover Square, in a year. But, of course all depends on the eye of the beholder.

TRANSFERABLE LIVES

I SOMETIMES have a fancy to speculate how, supposing the matter still undecided, I would like to spend my life. Often I feel how good it would be to give it in service to one of my six dear friends : just to offer it to them as so much capital, for whatever it may be worth. In pondering the fancy, I need hardly say that I do not assess myself at any extravagant value. I but venture to think that the devotion of one human creature, however humble, throughout a lifetime, is not a despicable offering. To use me as they would, to fetch and carry with me, to draw on me for whatever force resides in me, as they would on a bank account, to the last penny, to use my brains for their plans, my heart for their love, my blood for added length of days : and thus be so much the more true in their love, the more prosperous in their business, the more buoyant in their health—by the addition of *me*.

But then embarrassment comes upon me. Which of my friends do I love the most? To whose account of the six would I fain be credited? Then again I think of the ten thousand virgins, who go mateless about the world, sweet women, with hearts like hidden treasure, awaiting the 'Prince's kiss' that never comes ; virgin mothers, whose bosoms shall never know the light warm touch of baby-hands :

> ' Pale primroses
> That die unmarried, ere they can behold
> Bright Phœbus in his strength.'

How often one sees such a one in train or omnibus, her eyes, maybe, spilling the precious spikenard of their maternal love on some happier woman's child. I noticed one of them withering on the stalk, on my way to town this morning. She was, I surmised, nearly twenty-eight, she carried a roll of music, and I had a strong impression that she was the sole support of an invalid mother. I could hardly resist suggesting to one of my men companions, what a good

wife she was longing to make, what a
Sleeping Beauty she was, waiting for the
marital kiss that would set all the sweet bells
of her nature a-chime. I had the greatest
difficulty in preventing myself from leaning
over to her, and putting it to her in this way:

'Excuse me, madam, but I love you.
Will you be my wife? I am just turning
thirty. I have so much a year, a comfortable
little home, and probably another thirty
years of life to spend. Will you not go
shares with me?'

And my imagination went on making
pictures: how her eyes would suddenly
brighten up like the northern aurora, how
a strange bloom would settle on her somewhat weary face, and a dimple steal into her
chin; how, when she reached home and sat
down to read Jane Austen to her mother,
her mother would suddenly imagine roses in
the room, and she would blushingly answer,
'Nay, mother—it is my cheeks!'; and
presently the mother would ask, 'Where is
that smell of violets coming from?' and again
she would answer, 'Nay, mother—it is my
thoughts!'; and yet again the mother would

say, 'Hush! listen to that wonderful bird singing yonder!' and she would answer, 'Nay, mother dear—it is only my heart!'

But, alas, she alighted at Charing Cross, and not one of us in the compartment had asked her to be his wife.

The weary clerk, the sweated shopman, the jaded engineer—how good it would be to say to any of them, 'Here, let us change places awhile. Here is my latch-key, my cheque-book, my joy and my leisure. Use them as long as you will. Quick, let us change clothes, and let me take my share of the world's dreariness and pain.'

Or to stop the old man of sixty, as he hobbles down the hill, with never a thought of youth or spring in his heart, not a hope in his pocket, and his faith long since run dry— to stop him and say: 'See, here are thirty years; I have no use for them. Will you not take them? If you are quick, you may yet catch up Phyllis by the stile. She has a wonderful rose in her hand. She will sell it you for these thirty years; and she knows a field where a lark is singing as though it were in heaven!'

To take the old lady from the bath-chair,
and let her run with her daughter to gather
buttercups, or make eyes at the church
gallants.   Oh! this were better far than
living to oneself, if we were only selfish
enough to see it!

But, best of all were it to go to the
churchyard, where the dead have long since
given up all hopes of resurrection, and find
some new grave, whose inhabitant was not
yet so fast asleep but that he might be
awakened by a kind word.   To go to Alice's
grave and call, 'Alice! Alice!' and then
whisper : 'The spring is here!   Didn't you
hear the birds calling you ?   I have come to
tell you it is time to get ready.   In two
hours the church-bells will be ringing, and
Edward will be waiting for you at the altar.
The organist is already trying over the
'Wedding March,' and the bridesmaids have
had their dresses on and off twice.   They
can talk of nothing but orange-blossom and
rice.   Alice, dear, awaken.   Ah, did you
have strange dreams, poor girl—dream that
you were dead!   Indeed, it was a dream—
an evil dream.'

And, then, as Alice stepped bewildered homewards, to steal down into her place, and listen, and listen, till the sound of carriages rolled towards the gate, listen till the low hush of the marriage service broke into the wild happy laughter of the organ, and the babbling sound of sweet girls stole through the church porch; then to lie back and to think that Alice and Edward had been married after all—that your little useless life had been so much use; at least: just to dream of that awhile, and then softly fall asleep.

Ah, who would not give all his remaining days to ransom his beloved dead?—to give them the joys they missed, the hopes they clutched at, the dreams they dreamed. O river that runs so sweetly by their feet, when you shall have stopped running will they rise? O sun that shines above their heads, when you have ceased from shining will they come to us again? When the lark shall have done with singing, and the hawthorn bud no more, shall we then, indeed, hear the voices of our beloved, sweeter than song of river or bird?

THE APPARITION OF YOUTH

SENTENTIOUS people are fond of telling us that we change entirely every seven years, that in that time every single atomy of body (and soul?) finds a substitute. Personally, I am of opinion that we change oftener, that rather we are triennial in our constitution. In fact, it is a change we owe to our spiritual cleanliness. But there is a truth pertaining to the change of which the sententious people are not, I think, aware. When they speak of our sloughing our dead selves, they imagine the husk left behind as a dead length of hollow scale or skin. Would it were so. These sententious people, with all their information, have probably never gone through the process of which they speak. They have never changed from the beginning, but have been consistently their dull selves all through. To those, how-

ever, who can look back on many a meta-
morphosis, the quick-change artists of life,
a fearful thing is known. The length of discarded snake lies glistering in the greenwood,
motionless, and slowly perishes with the
fallen leaves in autumn. But for the dead
self is no autumn. By some mysterious
law of spiritual propagation, it breaks away
from us, a living thing, as the offspring of
primitive organisms are, it is said, broken off
the tail of their sole and undivided parent.
It goes on living as we go on living; often,
indeed if we be poets or artists, it survives us
many years; it may be a friend, but it is
oftener a foe; and it is always a sad
companion.

I sat one evening in my sumptuous
library near Rutland Gate. I was deep in
my favourite author, my bank-book, when
presently an entry—as a matter of fact, a
quarterly allowance to a friend (well, a
woman friend) of my youth—set me thinking. Just then my man entered. A youth
wished to see me. He would not give his
name, but sent word that I knew him very
well for all that. Being in a good humour, I

consented to see him. He was a young man of about twenty, and his shabby clothes could not conceal that he was comely. He entered the room with light step and chin in air, and to my surprise he strode over to where I sat and seated himself without a word. Then he looked at me with his blue eyes, and I recognised him with a start. 'What's the new book?' he asked eagerly, pointing to my open bank-book.

Bending over he looked at it: 'Pshaw! Figures. You used not to care much about them. When we were together it used to be Swinburne's *Poems and Ballads*, or Shakespeare's *Sonnets*!'

As he spoke, he tugged a faded copy of the *Sonnets* from his pocket. It slipped from his hand. As it fell it opened, and faded violets rained from its leaves. The youth gathered them up carefully, as though they had been valuable, and replaced them.

'How do you sell your violets?' I asked, ironically. 'I'll give you a pound apiece for them!'

'A pound! Twenty pounds apiece wouldn't buy them,' he laughed, and I remembered that they were the violets Alice Sunshine and I had gathered one spring day when I was twenty. We had found them in a corner of the dingle, where I had been reading the *Sonnets* to her, till in our book that day we read no more. As we parted she pressed them between the leaves and kissed them. I remember, too, that I had been particular to write the day and hour against them, and I remember further how it puzzled me a couple of years after what the date could possibly mean.

Having secured his book, my visitor once more looked me straight in the face, and as he did so he seemed to grow perplexed and disappointed. As I gazed at him my contentment, too, seemed to be slowly melting away. Five minutes before I had felt the most comfortable *bourgeois* in the world. There seemed nothing I was in need of, but there was something about this youth that was dangerously disillusionising. Here was I already envying him his paltry violets. I was even weak enough to offer him five pounds apiece for them, but he still smilingly shook his head.

'Well!' he said presently, 'what have you been doing with yourself all these years?'

I told him of my marriage and my partnership in a big city house.

'Phew!' he said. 'Monstrous dull, isn't it? As for me, I never intend to marry. And if you don't marry, what do you want with money? You used to despise it enough once. And do you remember our favourite line: *"Our loves into corpses or wives?"'*

'Hush!' I said, for wives have ears.

'Is it Alice Sunshine?' he asked.

'No,' I said, 'not Alice Sunshine.'

'Maud Willow?'

'No, not Maud Willow.'

'Jenny Hopkins?'

'No, not Jenny Hopkins.'

'Lucy Rainbow?'

'No, not Lucy Rainbow.'

'Now who else was there? I cannot remember them all. Ah, I remember now. It wasn't Lilian, after all?'

'No, poor Lilian died ten years ago. I am afraid you don't know my wife. I don't think you ever met.'

'It isn't Edith Appleblossom, surely? Is it'

'No, I . . .' and then I stopped just in time! 'No, you don't know my wife, I'm sure, and if you don't mind my saying so, I think I had better not introduce you. Forgive me, but she wouldn't quite understand you, I fear . . .'

'Wouldn't quite approve, eh?' said he, with a merry laugh. 'Poor old chap!'

'Well, I'm better off than that,' he continued. 'Why, Doll and I love for a week, and then forget each other's names in a twelvemonth, when Poll comes along, and so on. And neither of us is any the worse, believe me. We're one as fickle as the other, so where's the harm?'

'Ah, my dear fellow, you did make a mistake,' he ran on. 'I suppose you forget Robert Louis' advice—"*Times are changed with him who marries,*" etc.'

'He's married himself,' I replied.

'And I suppose you never drop in for a pipe at "The Three Tuns" now of an evening?'

'No! I haven't been near the place these many years.'

'Poor old fellow! The Bass is superb at present.

I recollected. 'Won't you have some wine
with me?' I said. 'I have some fine old
Chianti. And take a cigar?'

'No, thanks, old man. I'm too sad.
Come with me to "The Three Tuns," and
let's have an honest pint and an honest pipe
together. I don't care about cigars. Come
to-night. Let's make a night of it. We'll
begin at "The Three Tuns," then call at
"The Blue Posts," look in at "The Dog and
Fire-irons," and finish up at "The Shakespeare's Head." What was it we used to
troll?—

> ' From tavern to tavern
>   Youth passes along,
>   With an armful of girl
>   And a heart-full of song.' "

'Hush!' I cried in terror; 'it is impossible.
I cannot. Come to my club instead.' But
he shook his head.

I persuaded him to have some Chianti at
last, but he drank it without spirit, and thus
we sat far into the night talking of old days.

Before he went I made him a definite offer
—he must have bewitched me, I am sure—
I offered him no less than £5,000 and a share

in the business for the sprig of almond-blossom the ridiculous young pagan carried in his hat.

And will you believe me? He declined the offer.

THE PATHETIC FLOURISH

THE dash under the signature, the unnecessary rat-tat of the visitor, the extravagant
angle of the hat in bowing, the extreme
unction in the voice, the business man's
importance, the strut of the cock, the swagger
of the bad actor, the long hair of the poet,
the Salvation bonnet, the blue shirt of the
Socialist : against all these, and a hundred
examples of the swagger of unreflecting life,
did a little brass knocker in Gray's Inn warn
me the other evening. I had knocked as
no one should who is not a postman, with
somewhat of a flourish. I had plainly said,
in its metallic reverberations, that I was some-
body. As I left my friends, I felt the knocker
looking at me, and when I came out into the
great square, framing the heavens like an
astronomical chart, the big stars repeated the
lesson with thousand-fold iteration. How

they seemed to nudge each other and twinkle among themselves at the poor ass down there, who actually took himself and his doings so seriously as to flourish, even on a little brass knocker.

Yes, I had once again forgotten Jupiter. How many hundred times was he bigger than the earth? Never mind, there he was, bright as crystal, for me to measure my importance against! The street-lamps did their best, I observed, to brave it out, and the electric lights in Holborn seemed certainly to have the best of it—as cheap jewellery is gaudiest in its glitter. One could much more easily believe that all these hansoms with their jewelled eyes, these pretty, saucily frocked women with theirs, this busy glittering milky way of human life was the enduring, and those dimmed uncertain points up yonder but the reflections of human gas-lights.

A city clerk, with shining evening hat, went by, his sweetheart on his arm. They were wending gaily to the theatre, without a thought of all the happy people who had done the same long ago—hasting down the self-same street, to the self-same theatre, with

the very same sweet talk—all long since
mouldering in their graves. I felt I ought to
rush up and shake them, take them into a by-
street, turn their eyes upon Jupiter, and tell
them they must die ; but I thought it might
spoil the play for them.

Besides, there were so many hundreds in
the streets I should have to address in the
same way : formidable people, too, clad in re-
spectability as in a coat of mail. The pomp-
ous policeman yonder : I longed to go and
say to him that there had been policemen
before ; that he was only the ephemeral
example of a world-old type, and needn't
take himself so seriously. It was an irresis-
tible temptation to ask him : 'Canst thou
bind the sweet influences of Pleiades, or
loose the bands of Orion ? Canst thou bring
forth Mazzaroth in his season ? Or canst
thou guide Arcturus with his sons ?' But I
forbore, and just then, glancing into an oyster
shop, I was fascinated by the oysterman. He
was rapidly opening a dozen for a new
customer, and wore the while the solemnest
face I ever saw. Oysters were so evidently,
so pathetically, all the world to him. All his

surroundings suggested oysters, legends of their prices and qualities made the art on his walls, printed price-lists on his counter made his literature, the prospects and rivalries of trade made his politics : oysters were, in fact, his *raison d'être.* His associations from boyhood had been oysters, I felt certain that his relatives, even his ancestors, must be oysters, too ; and that if he had any idea of a supreme being, it must take the form of an oyster. Indeed, a sort of nightmare seemed suddenly to take possession of the world, in which alternately policemen swallowed oysters and oysters policemen. How sad it all was—that masterly flourish of the knife with which the oysterman ruthlessly hurried dozen after dozen into eternity ; that defer-ential ' Sir ' in his voice to every demand of his customer ; that brisk alacrity with which he bid his assistant bring 'the gentleman's half-stout.'

There seemed a world of tears in these simple operations, and the plain oysterman had grown suddenly mystical as an astro-logical symbol. And, indeed, there was planetary influence in the thing, for there was Jupiter high above us, sneering at our little world of policemen and oystermen.

His grin disagreeably reminded me—had I not myself that very night ignorantly flourished on a brass knocker?

It is so hard to remember the respect we owe to death. Yet for me there is always a feeling that if we direct our lives cautiously, with proportionate seriousness and no more, not presuming on life as our natural birthright, but taking it with simple thankfulness as a boon which we have done nothing to deserve, and which may be snatched from us before our next breath : that, if we so order our days, Death may respect our humility.

> ' The lusty lord, rejoicing in his pride,
>   He draweth down ; before the armèd knight
> With jingling bridle-rein he still doth ride ;
>   He crosseth the strong captain in the fight ';

but such are proud people, arrogant in beauty and strength. With a humble person, who is careful not to flourish beneath his signature, who knocks just as much as he means on the knocker, bows just as much as he respects, smiles cautiously, and never fails to touch his hat to the King of Terrors—may he not deal more gently with such a one?

And yet Death is not a pleasant companion at Life's feast, however kindly disposed. One cannot quite trust him, and he doesn't go well with flowers. Perhaps, after all, they are wisest who forget him, and happy indeed are they who have not yet caught sight of him grinning to himself among the green branches of their Paradise.

Yes, it is good that youth should go with a feather in his cap, that spring should garland herself with blossom, and love's vows make light of death. He is a bad companion for young people. But for older folk the wisdom of that knocker in Gray's Inn applies.

A TAVERN NIGHT

LOOKING back, in weak moments, we are sometimes heard to say: 'After all, youth was a great fool. Look at the tinsel he was sure was solid gold. Can you imagine it? This tawdry tinkling bit of womanhood, a silly doll that says " Don't" when you squeeze it, —he actually mistook her for a goddess.' Ah! reader, don't you wish you could make such a splendid mistake? I do. I'd give anything to be once more sitting before the footlights for the first time, with the wonderful overture just beginning to steal through my senses.

Ah! violins, whither would you take my soul? You call to it like the voice of one waiting by the sea, bathed in sunset. Why do you call me? What are these wonderful things you are whispering to my soul? You promise—ah! what things you promise, strange voices of the string!

184

O sirens, have pity! It is the soul of a boy comes out to meet you. His heart is pure, his body sweet as apples. Oh, be faithful, betray him not, beautiful voices of the wondrous world!

David and I sat together in a theatre. The overture had succeeded. Our souls had followed it over the footlights, and, floating in the limelight, shone there awaiting the fulfilment of the promise. The play was 'Pygmalion and Galatea.' I almost forget now how the scenes go, I only know that at the appearance of Galatea we knew that the overture had not lied. There, in dazzling white flesh, was all it had promised; and when she called 'Pyg-ma-lion!' how our hearts thumped! for we knew it was really us she was calling.

'Pyg-ma-lion!' 'Pyg-ma-lion!'

It was as though Cleopatra called us from the tomb.

Our hands met. We could hear each other's blood singing. And was not the play itself an allegory of our coming lives? Did not Galatea symbolise all the sleeping beauty of the world that was to awaken

warm and fragrant at the kiss of our youth?
And somewhere, too, shrouded in enchanted
quiet, such a white white woman waited for
our kiss.

In a vision we saw life like the treasure
cave of the Arabian thief, and we said to
our beating hearts that we had the secret of
the magic word : that the 'Open Sesame'
was youth.

No fall of the curtain could hide the vision
from our young eyes. It transfigured the
faces of our fellow-pittites, it made another
stage of the embers of the sunset, a distant
bridge of silver far down the street. Then we
took it with us to the tavern : and, as I think
of the solemn libations of that night, I know
not whether to laugh or cry. Doubtless, you
will do the laughing and I the crying.

We had got our own corner. Turning
down the gas, the fire played at day and
night with our faces. Imagine us in one of
the flashes, solemnly raising our glasses,
hands clasped across the table, earnest
gleaming eyes holding each other above it.
'Old man! some day, somewhere, a woman
like that!'

There was still a sequel. At home at last and in bed, how could I sleep? It seemed as if I had got into a rosy sunset cloud in mistake for my bed. The candle was out, and yet the room was full of rolling light.

I'll swear I could have seen to read by it, whatever it was.

It was no use. I must get up. I struck a light, and in a moment was deep in the composition of a fiery sonnet. It was evidently that which had caused all the phosphorescence. But a sonnet is a mere pill-box. It holds nothing. A mere cockle-shell. And, oh! the raging sea it could not hold! Besides, being confessedly an art-form, duly licensed to lie, it is apt to be misunderstood. It could not say in plain English, 'Meet me at the pier to-morrow at three in the afternoon'; it could make no assignation nearer than the Isles of the Blest, 'after life's fitful fever.' Therefore, it seemed well to add a postscript to that effect in prose.

And then, how was she to receive it? Needless to say, there was nothing to be hoped from the post; and I should have said before that Tyre and Sidon face each other on opposite sides of the river, and that my home was in Sidon, three miles from the ferry.

Likewise, it was now nearing three in the morning. Just time to catch the half-past three boat, run up to the theatre, a mile away, and meet the return boat. So down down through the creaking house, gingerly, as though I were a Jason picking my way among the coils of the sleeping dragon. Soon I was shooting along the phantom streets, like Mercury on a message through Hades.

At last the river came in sight, growing slate-colour in the earliest dawn. I could see the boat nuzzling up against the pier, and snoring in its sleep. I said to myself that this was Styx and the fare an obolus. As I jumped on board, with hot face and hotter heart, Charon clicked his signal to the engines, the boat slowly snuffled itself half awake, and we shoved out into the sleepy water.

As we crossed, the light grew, and the gas-lamps of Tyre beaconed with fading gleam.

Overhead began a restlessness in the clouds,
as of a giant drowsily shuffling off some of
his bedclothes ; but as yet he slept, and only
the silver bosom of his spouse the moon was
uncovered.

When we landed, the streets of Tyre were
already light, but empty : as though they
had got up early to meet some one who had
not arrived. I sped through them like a sea-
gull that has the harbour to itself, and was
not long in reaching the theatre. How
desolate the playbills looked that had been
so companionable but two or three hours before. And there was her photograph !
Surely it was an omen. Ah, my angel !
See, I am bringing you my heart in a song
'All my heart in this my singing !'

I dropped the letter into the box : but, as
I turned away, momentarily glancing up the
long street, I caught sight of an approaching
figure that could hardly be mistaken. Good
Heavens ! it was David, and he too was
carrying a letter.

SANDRA BELLONI'S
PINEWOOD

(TO THE SWEET MEMORY OF FRANCES WYNNE)

I FELT jaded and dusty, I needed flowers
and sunshine ; and remembering that some
one had told me—erroneously, I have since
discovered !—that the pinewood wherein
Sandra Belloni used to sing to her harp,
like a nixie, in the moonlit nights, lay near
Oxshott in Surrey, I vowed myself there
and then to the Meredithian pilgrimage.
The very resolution uplifted me with lyric
gladness, and I went swinging out of the old
Inn where I live with the heart of a boy.
Across Lincoln's Inn Fields, down by the
Law Courts, and so to Waterloo. I felt I
must have a confidante, so I told the slate-
coloured pigeons in the square where I was
off—out among the thrushes, the broom,
and the may. But they wouldn't come.

They evidently deemed that a legal purlieu was a better place for 'pickings.'

Half-a-crown return to Oxshott and a train at 12.35. You know the ride better than I, probably, and what Surrey is at the beginning of June. The first gush of green on our getting clear of Clapham was like the big drink after an afternoon's hay-making. There was but one cloud on the little journey. She got into the next carriage.

I dreamed all the way. On arriving at Oxshott I immediately became systematic. Having a very practical belief in the material basis of all exquisite experience, I simply nodded to the great pinewoods half a mile off, on the brow of long heathy downs to the left of the railway bridge—as who should say, 'I shall enjoy you all the better presently for some sandwiches and a pint of ale'—and promptly, not to say scientifically, turned down the Oxshott road in search of an inn.

Oxshott is a quaint little hamlet, one of the hundred villages where we are going to live when we have written great novels ; but

I didn't care for the village inn, so walked a quarter of a mile nearer Leatherhead, till the Old Bear came in sight.

There I sat in the drowsy parlour, the humming afternoon coming in at the door, 'the blue fly' singing on the hot pane, dreaming all kinds of gauzy-winged dreams, while my body absorbed ham sandwiches and some excellent ale. Of course I did not leave the place without the inevitable reflection on Lamb and the inns *he* had immortalised. Outside again my thoughts were oddly turned to the nature of my expedition by two figures in the road—an unhappy-looking couple, evidently 'belonging to each other,' the young woman with babe at breast, trudging together side by side—

> 'One was a girl with a babe that throve,
>   Her ruin and her bliss;
> One was a youth with a lawless love,
>   Who claspt it the more for this.'

The quotation was surely inevitable for any one who knows Mr. Meredith's tragic little picture of 'The Meeting.'

Thus I was brought to think of Sandra again, and of the night when the Brookfield ladies had heard her singing like a spirit in the heart of the moon-dappled pinewood, and impresario Pericles had first prophesied the future prima donna.

Do you remember his inimitable outburst?—'I am made my mind! I send her abroad to ze Académie for one, two, tree year. She shall be instructed as was not before. Zen a noise at La Scala. No—Paris! No—London! She shall astonish London fairst. Yez! if I take a theatre! Yez! if I buy a newspaper! Yez! if I pay feefty-sossand pound!'

Of course, as one does, I had gone expecting to distinguish the actual sandy mound among the firs where she sat with her harp, the young countryman waiting close by for escort, and the final 'Giles Scroggins, native British, beer-begotten air' with which she rewarded him for his patience in suffering so much classical music. Mr. Meredith certainly gives a description of the spot close enough for identification, with time and perseverance. But, reader, I had gone out this afternoon in the interest rather of fresh air than of sentimental topography; and it was

N

quite enough for me to feel that somewhere in that great belt of pinewood it had all been true, and that it was through those fir-branches and none other in the world that that 'sleepy fire of early moonlight' had so wonderfully hung.

After crossing the railway bridge the road rises sharply for a few yards, and then a whole stretch of undulating woodland is before one: to the right bosky green, but on the left a rough dark heath with a shaggy wilderness of pine for background, heightened here and there with a sudden surprise of gentle silver birch. How freshly the wind met one at the top of the road: a south-west wind soft and blithe enough to have blown through 'Diana of the Crossways.'

'You saucy south wind, setting all the budded beech
    boughs swinging
Above the wood anemones that flutter, flushed and white,
When far across the wide salt waves your quick way you
    were winging,
Oh! tell me, tell me, did you pass my sweetheart's ship last
    night?
            Ah! let the daisies be,
            South wind! and answer me;
            Did you my sailor see?
            Wind, whisper very low,
            For none but you must know
            I love my lover so.'

I had been keeping that question to ask it
for two or three days, since a good friend
had told me of some lyrics by Miss Frances
Wynne; and the little volume, charmingly
entitled *Whisper*, was close under my arm
as I turned from the road across the heath—
a wild scramble of scrubby chance-children,
wind-sown from the pines behind. And
then presently, like a much greater person,
'I found me in a gloomy wood astray.'

But I soon realised that it wasn't the day
for pinewoods, however rich in associations.
Dark days are their opportunity. Then one
is in sympathy. But on days when the
sunshine is poured forth like yellow wine,
when the broom is ablaze, and the sky blue
as particular eyes, the contrast of those dark
aisles without one green blade is uncanny.
Its listening loneliness almost frightens one.
Brurrhh! One must find a greenwood where
things are companionable : birds within call,
butterflies in waiting, and a bee now and
again to bump one, and be off again with
a grumbled 'Beg your pardon. Confound
you!' So presently imagine me 'prone at
the foot of yonder' sappy chestnut, nice little

cushions of moss around me, one for *Whisper*, one for a pillow ; above, a world of luminous green leaves, filtered sunlight lying about in sovereigns and half-sovereigns, and at a distance in the open shine a patch of hyacinths, 'like a little heaven below.'

Whisper! 'Tis, the sweetest little book of lyrics since Mrs. Dollie Radford's *Light Load*. Whitman, you will remember, always used to take his songs out into the presence of the fields and skies to try them. A severe test, but a little book may bear it as well as a great one. The *Leaves of Grass* claims measurement with oaks; but *Whisper* I tried by speedwell and cinquefoil, and many other tiny sweet things for which I know no name, by all airs and sounds coming to me through the wood, quaint little notes of hidden birds,—and the songs were just as much at home there as the rest, because they also had grown out of Nature's heart, and were as much hers as any leaf or bird. So I dotted speedwell all amongst them, because I felt they ought to know each other.

I wonder if you love to fill your books

with flowers. It is a real bookish delight,
and they make such a pretty diary. My
poets are full of them, and they all mean a
memory—old spring mornings, lost sunsets,
walks forgotten and unforgotten. Here a
buttercup pressed like finely beaten brass,
there a great yellow rose—in my Keats; my
Chaucer is like his old meadows, 'ypoudred
with daisie,' and my Herrick is full of violets.
The only thing is that they haunt me
sometimes. But then, again, they bloom
afresh every spring. As Mr. Monkhouse
sings :—

'Sweet as the rose that died last year is the rose that is
    born to-day.'

But I grow melancholy with an Englishman's
afterthought, for I coined no such reflections
dreaming there in the wood. It is only on
paper that one moralises—just where one
shouldn't.

My one or two regrets were quite practical
—that I had not learnt botany at school, and
that the return train went so early.

WHITE SOUL

WHAT is so white in the world, my love,
As thy maiden soul—
The dove that flies
Softly all day within thine eyes,
And nests within thine heart at night ?
Nothing so white.

ONE has heard poets speak of a quill
dropped from an angel's wing. That is the
kind of nib of which I feel in need to-night.
If I could but have it just for to-night only,
—I would willingly bequeath it to the British
Museum to-morrow. As a rule I am very
well satisfied with the particular brand of gilt
' J' with which I write to the dictation of the
Muse of Daily Bread ; but to-night it is
different. Though it come not, I must make
ready to receive a loftier inspiration. Whitest
paper, newest pen, ear sensitive, tremulous ;
heart pure and mind open, broad and clear as
the blue air for the most delicate gossamer
thoughts to wing through ; and snow-white
words, lily-white words, words of ivory and

pearl, words of silver and alabaster, words white as hawthorn and daisy, words white as morning milk, words 'whiter than Venus' doves, and softer than the down beneath their wings.'—virginal, saintlike, nunnery words.

It may be because I love White Soul that I think her the fairest blossom on the Tree of Life, yet a child said of her to its mother, the other day : ' Look at White Soul's face—it is as though it were lit up from inside !' Children, if they don't always tell the truth, seldom tell lies ; and I always think that the praise of children is better worth having than the Cross of the Legion of Honour. They are the only critics from whom praise is not to be bought. As animals are said to see spirits, children have, I think, an eye for souls. It is so easy to have an eye for beautiful surfaces. Such eyes are common enough. An eye for beautiful souls is rarer ; and, unless you possess that eye for souls, you waste your time on White Soul. She has, of course, her external attractions, dainty features, refined contours ; but these it would not be difficult to match in any morning's walk. It is when she smiles that her face, it seems to me, is one of the most wonderful in the world. Till she smiles, it is like the score of some great composer's song before the musician releases it warbling for joy along the trembling keys; it is like the statue of Memnon before the dawn steals to kiss it across the desert. White Soul's face when she smiles is made, you would say, of larks and dew, of nightingales and stars.

She is an eldritch little creature, a little frightening to live with—with her gold flaxen hair that seems to grow blonder as it nears her head: burnt blonde, it would seem, with the white light of the spirit that pours all day long from her brows. There is something, as we say, almost supernatural about her—'a fairy's child.' The gipsies have a share in her blood, she boasts in her naïve way, and with her love for all that is free and lawless and under-the-sky—but I always say the fairies have more. She is constantly saying 'Hush!' and 'Whisht!' when no one else can hear a sound, and she dreams the quaintest of dreams.

Once she woke sobbing in the night and told her husband, who knew her ways and

loved her tenfold for them, that she had
dreamed herself in the old churchyard, and
that as the moon rose behind the tower, the
three old men who live in the three yew-trees
had come out and played cards upon a tomb
in the moonlight, and one of them had
beckoned to her and offered to tell her fortune.
It fell out that she was to die in the spring,
and as he held up the fatal card, the old man
had leered at her—and then a cock crew,
all three vanished, and she awoke.

Her dreams are nearly all about dying, and,
though she is obviously robust, there is that
transparent ethereal look in her face, which
makes old women say 'she is not long for
this world,' that fateful beauty which creates
an atmosphere of doom about it. You cannot
look at her without a queer involuntary feeling that she was born to die in some tragic
way. She reminds one of those perilously
fragile vases we feel must get broken, those
rarely delicate flowers we feel cannot have
strong healthy roots.

She is one of those who seem born to see
terrible things, monstrous accidents, supernatural appearances. She has seen death

and birth in strange uncanny forms ; and
she has met with unearthly creatures in the
lonely corners of rooms. She is a ' seventh-
month child,' and ' seventh-month children '
always see things,' she says, with a funny
little sententious shake of her head.

Yet, with all this, she is the sunniest, healthi-
est, most domestic little soul that breathes ;
and no doubt the materialist would be right in
saying that all this ' spirituelle ' nonsense is
but a trick of her transparent blonde complexion, a chance quality in the colour of
her great luminous eyes.

Like all women, she was most wonderful
just before the birth of her first child, a
little changeling creature wild-eyed as her
fairy mother. How she made believe with
the little fairy vestments, the elfin-shirts,
the pixy-frocks—long before it was time for
the tiny body to step inside them ; how she
talked to the unborn soul that none but she
as yet could see. And all the time she ' knew '
she was going to die, that she would never
see the little immortal that was about to put
on our mortality : ' people ' had told her so
in her dreams at night,—doubtless ' the good

people,' the fairies. Those who loved her
grew almost to believe her—she looks so like
a little Sibyl when she says such things—yet
her little one came almost without a cry, and
in a few days the fairy mother was once more
glinting about the house like a sunbeam.

Well! well! I cannot make you see her
as I know her : that I fear is certain. You
might meet her, yet never know her from my
description. If you wait for the coarse arti-
culation of words you might well ' miss ' her ;
for her qualities are not histrionic, they have
no notion of making the best of themselves.
They remain, so to speak, in nuggets ; they
are minted into no current coin of fleeting
fashion and shallow accomplishment. But if
a face can mean more to you than the whole
of Johnson's *Dictionary*, and the *Encyclopædia
Britannica* to boot, if a strain of music can
convey to you the thrill of human life, with its
heights and depths and romantic issues and
possibilities, as Gibbon and Grote can never
do—come and worship White Soul's face with
me. Some women's faces are like diamonds
—they look their best in artificial lights ;
White Soul's face is bright with the soft

brightness of a flower—a flower tumbled with dew, and best seen in the innocent lights of dawn. Dear face without words!

And if there are those who can look on that face without being touched by its strange spiritual loveliness, without seeing in it one of those clear springs that bubble up from the eternal beauty, there must indeed be many who would miss the soul for which her face is but the ivory gate, who would never know how white is all within, never see or hear that holy dove.

But I have seen and heard, and I know that if God should covet White Soul and steal her from me, her memory would ever remain with me as one of those eternal realities of the spirit to which 'realities' of flesh and blood, of wood and stone, are but presumptuous shadows.

I am not worthy of White Soul. Indeed, just to grow more worthy of her was I put into the world.

www.ingramcontent.com/pod-product-compliance
Lightning Source LLC
Chambersburg PA
CBHW030825270326

41928CB00007B/905